HOW TO SURVIVE
CRAZY

*Partners, Family, Friends, Employers,
Coworkers, Situations, and Life*

TRISH BAGWELL

How to Survive Crazy

Trilogy Christian Publishers
A Wholly Owned Subsidary of Trinity Broadcasting Network
2442 Michelle Drive, Tustin, CA 92780

Trilogy Christian Publishing/TBN and colophon are trademarks of Trinity Broadcasting Network.

For information about special discounts for bulk purchases, please contact Trilogy Christian Publishing.

Trilogy Disclaimer: The views and content expressed in this book are those of the author and may not necessarily reflect the views and doctrine of Trilogy Christian Publishing or the Trinity Broadcasting Network.

Manufactured in the United States of America
10 9 8 7 6 5 4 3 2 1
Library of Congress Cataloging-in-Publication Data is available.

ISBN: 979-8-88738-667-6
E-ISBN: 979-8-88738-668-3

DEDICATION

To My Three Beautiful Children

First and foremost, I would like to dedicate this book to them. Thank you for loving me during, through, and after all the trying times; we have made it through… together!

I love each of you dearly and hope that you have each learned something valuable in what we have experienced together that will serve to alleviate hardships for you.

Thank you for lovingly supporting and encouraging me through this endeavor and trusting, without reading it first, that I will make you proud of my work.

To My Loving Mentor and Her Husband, Too

Thank you both for being there for me through many trying times, even if I called at five o'clock in the morning needing someone to listen and care!

Thank you both for loving, praying, and mentoring me through not only this book but my life since I met you. You are both very special to me.

Thank you both for being my editors and allowing me to finish my book without questioning or making me feel that I said too much or not enough but encouraging me through it!

To My Prayer Warriors

To all my prayer warriors who have been in prayer for this book for the six months I gave myself to write it!

To one special prayer warrior for always going out of her way to let me know that I would succeed and for all her kind and loving encouragement!

To My Friends

To all my friends who have been willing to help me and those who have been willing to encouragingly listen while I shared with them some of the stories that I have included in this book!

To two special dear friends I worked with in the past that actually made me understand the meaning of my dream as well as my heart. (You will read that story later in the book entitled *Borrowed Mattresses and Pictures Returned*.)

To My Family

Last but not least, thank you for all you have been through with me, supported me through, and encouraged me through.

TABLE OF CONTENTS

PROLOGUE

This book that I have written to share with the world is a synopsis of my life, beginning with my childhood. I take you through the tumultuous journey of living in an abusive household and share many perplexing stories that caused not only me but also some of my siblings to struggle as both children and adults to understand how and why things happened.

I also describe the many hardships and choices that I made in my youth that may have been impacted by the things that were missing growing up.

In the sixth grade, I was introduced to church by my classmate who was mentoring me in math. However, this introduction came with a lot of intimidation due to the fact that I knew nothing about church or the Bible, and my friend seemed to know everything.

Because of this introduction in the sixth grade, and I am now sixty-two, I have had a beautiful and powerful spiritual journey. I have grown to cherish the times and moments in my life that have not only inspired but caused the experiences I have had and brought me to and through many things. Because of the challenges, hardships, hurt, pain, anguish, and bad choices that I have made, it has caused me to search for something greater. Something more powerful than all those things… and I can honestly say I have found it due to the trials, tribulations, and hardships I have endured.

My marriages, my family, my coworkers, my friends, and just life in general have been a roller coaster ride that I didn't want to go on, but nevertheless, I did. Some were choices that I made, and some were what I call "happenstance," but all had a huge impact on me.

The most important message that I hope to interject into your life is that we are all human; we all make mistakes, and we have the power to both choose our destiny and choose our path to take both in and through this life. While we may take many wrong turns along the way, we truly have the ultimate choice to make regarding how and who we choose to be and be with.

I have now chosen to be who I believe I was created to be! I believe I was created to experience what I have experienced in this life, what I have endured in this life, what I have overcome in this life, and to be who I am in Christ and what I believe He wants me to be...

In Christ! Amen!

Perhaps this is the moment for which you were created.

— Esther 4:14

INTRODUCTION

My story begins in the 1950s.

- I was the fourth child born in 1956 to a family of six children.
- There were two girls and four boys.
- The oldest child was my sister, six years older than me.
- Two brothers between my sister and me, and two brothers after me.
- There was a two-year age difference between all six of us.
- My mom was a homemaker in our early years.
- My dad was always a truck driver.
- My memories of childhood are not what one would think childhood memories ought to be about.
- Unfortunately, my most prevalent childhood memories are about fear, humility, pain, hurt, betrayal, and stress.
- In the later part of my youth, my most prevalent memories also include hard work to go along with the rest.
- I remember very little fun, laughter, and all the things that childhood memories ought to be about, within your family, but especially with your parents.
- You may notice that love was not on the list of all the things that childhood memories ought to be about… that's because I never felt, experienced, or remembered being or feeling loved and honestly knew nothing about it or what it meant for many years.

CHAPTER 1

212 Robert Avenue

1956–1965: Birth Through Third Grade

My one and only real pleasant family memory from early childhood is going on a family vacation with another family to some mountains. The Blue Ridge Parkway rings a bell, but I can't say for sure that's where we went. One day we got to stay in some cabins; it may have been a few days; I just remember that it was something altogether new and different. The most impressionable and pleasant memory is I got to stay in a cabin with the other family that went with us. I was so excited because they were different, and I got to have fun. Another fond memory is one day we got to eat out, at a hamburger place, and we didn't have to eat Spam that day! For those of you who have never heard of Spam, it is a canned meat (a substitute for ham, maybe) that was used on our vacation, I assume, as a quick, easy, and inexpensive way to feed eight people—every day with the exception of the one-day hamburger treat. I guess in those days, and with the salary my dad made, it was a way of being able to afford to take all eight of us on a family vacation and feed us at the same time. I think we went with another family so they could bring some of us kids so there was room for everyone.

I also think back on those days and wonder how we were even all able to fit into a car to go anywhere together, considering in those days the biggest vehicle wasn't even invented yet, I don't think, which may have been a "woodie" station wagon. A woodie was a car with wood on the side, and when you saw one, you were supposed to hit someone and call out "woodie" before they saw it and hit you. Little do some people know this was a game way before the VW Beetle game. Maybe it was a car then, and that is how all eight of us got around… can't say I remember our car.

So, I'm not really sure how we were all able to travel together unless we walked, of course, which was how we got to school. We lived in small-town USA in College Park, Georgia, right in front of the Atlanta airport. Lying in my bed at night, I could hear airplanes landing and instructions coming from the loudspeakers! Our address was 212 Robert Avenue. Sounds like a song, but there wasn't singing coming from our small little kitchen and living room, two bedrooms and one bathroom dwelling that eight people lived in.

Just imagine, if you can, two small bedrooms and one bathroom for eight people. The entire dwelling was probably no more than eight hundred square feet. Mom and Dad, of course, had one small bedroom, unless we were babies, and all six of us kids shared the other small bedroom. Two full-size beds lined two walls with just enough room to walk between the two beds. My sister and I shared one bed, and my next to the oldest brother and two younger brothers shared the other. My oldest brother got to have a twin-sized bed all his own at the other end of the room because he was sick with asthma. He got to have a dog to sleep with him, though. The dog, we were told, was to help with the asthma. It was a small bedroom, to begin with, and with two full-size beds and one twin, there was hardly room enough for a dresser to put all six of our clothes in. On school mornings, the rule was whichever gender hit the floor first got the room to change first. So, if one of the boy's feet hit the floor before one of the girl's feet hit the floor, then they got the room to be able to dress for school first. For some reason, that made it very important to be able to be the first gender for your feet to hit the floor. Not sure now why it mattered, but it did. As with any made-up rule, I'm sure there were disagreements, in the beginning, about who touched the floor first. But I'm also sure we learned that it really didn't matter who hit the floor first, just so long as we all got up and got dressed without fussing 'bout who won 'cause that would result in something that none of us would want the outcome that would follow.

Yes, fear, humility, and stress are some of the memories of my childhood while surviving at 212 Robert Avenue. You see, as I told you earlier, my mom, or Mama, as we called her, was a homemaker and my dad, or Diddy, as we called him, was a truck driver who would be gone for days at a time with his job. That left my Mama to handle all six of us kids while Diddy was away for long periods of time. If ever we didn't mind or got out of hand in any way, Mama wouldn't punish us right then, our punishment as Mama would say, "Just wait 'til your Diddy gets home." That was more punishment than if we had gotten a paddling, or a spanking, or a hickory switch from Mama, "The Wait." The punishment that Diddy dished out when he got home was something that caused all of us to wish upon our Diddy that he wouldn't make it home, even if that meant that he died. He always made it home, even though we agreed as a group that he wouldn't or that we didn't want him to. This is how I learned about fear, humility, and stress. You see, Diddy could fly off the handle in a minute, and before you knew what was happening, someone or anyone of the kids would either be getting a belt whooping or a toy or any multiple of things thrown at them or across the room. A belt whooping, which is what you got when Diddy got home, was not just a lick or two; it was kinda like a merry-go-round, but instead of a merry-go-round it was a "child-go-round" and round, and round, and round, and round, and round the room screaming and crying all the while with my Diddy holding their arm as they ran while using his other strong and pow-erful arm to lay belt lash, after lash, after lash, no matter the crying, or the begging and pleas of the recipient for him to stop. Seemingly to me, this went on forever. I can't begin to imagine how long it seemed to my siblings who were on the receiving end of the lashes.

I can't say, though, that I was ever the recipient of one of those whoopings because, for some reason, I was chosen by my Diddy as his favorite child. I did, however, feel the fear, humility, and stress, with the exception of the pain and hurt to the physical body, but I felt the pain and hurt to my heart that occurred when these encounters happened. I can recall watching one of these whoopings happening as I sat in the corner, as far back in the corner as I could get, of our small five-room dwelling at 212 Robert Avenue. I can remember being so very scared and wanting to help but knowing there was nothing I could do but make sure I wasn't next. I learned, thinking to myself, that I never wanted to get one of those whoopings, and so I decided, right then and there at a very young age, that I would just always be good! There was one thing I never could understand, though. I never understood why my Mama didn't take punishment matters into her own hands every time instead of allowing this to happen. Although many times it seems she would use that line, "Just wait 'til your Diddy gets home," to instill fear upon us so we wouldn't misbehave. Even the times when we had to go find our own hickory switch for her to use on us didn't leave the everlasting scars that the punishment that Diddy gave. I can only remember how hard it was to go find your own switch to be punished with and the sting of the switch, but not the scars it left. I guess it depended on the degree of misbehavior or her frustration with all six of us as to whether Diddy was actually told or not. But to me, nothing any of us did was bad enough to justify this…

I began writing this book on August 17, 2014, and today it is August 26, 2015.

It has taken me one year to get over the suppression that reliving these memories caused.

Now a year and a few days later, I am ready to finish this story that began at 212 Robert Avenue.

… happening. I suppose when I think about it now, as an adult, it could be the reason that I never felt or had a deep bond with my Mama—nor my Diddy. Don't get me wrong, even though I believe as children we were treated very badly, I still cared for my parents but never felt loved as a child, even though… supposedly I was the favorite; therefore, that parent-child bond was missing. Instead of that bond you should have, there was a feeling of fear, humility, mistrust, and stress, which I believe, in my little mind, was also a feeling of dismay and betrayal. I can honestly say I have very few pleasant memories at 212 Robert Avenue. Don't remember Christmas or any fun indoor things that happened. But we children spent lots of time outside with one another as that was an all day, every day, requirement except for my oldest brother, who has asthma, so he was allowed to stay inside.

I can remember an instance where my Diddy was mad at my brother, two years younger than me, and took his toy gun and rammed it through the bedroom door. There was a lot of rage and anger that went along with the gun being broken, and I never understood what or why this happened. Still don't know today, but I remember it happening. Another time when I'm sure I backed myself into the corner, as far as I could go into the corner, at 212 Robert Avenue.

I look back now on all the times that my Diddy would lose his temper and wonder if it was because of the big jar of pills that were kept in the cabinet above the stove that we kids were not supposed to touch and that he would sell or give, not sure, to other truck drivers or men sometimes. You see, all of us kids knew about this forbidden jar of pills, and we also knew other men would come and get them sometimes… but we also knew we had better never touch them. I always wondered what they were. They were kinda like the secret pads that were in the bathroom. But I was able to pick that box up and read it but still never could quite figure out the purpose. The intrigue for me was the secrecy that surrounded both the pills and the box of pads, which of course I now know what the pads were for. Now, I believe, I also know what the jar of pills' purpose was, although they have never been discussed with Mama or Diddy, just like all the other things that happened at 212 Robert Avenue. In sharing this pill story with an acquaintance, they said that truck drivers used to take a lot of speed to stay awake on their trips. It makes complete sense to me, and now it makes even more sense about why my Diddy may have acted the way he did. It also makes it easier to rationalize his behavior… at this age. As a child, there was no rationalizing, understanding, or justification… only agony, hurt, mistrust, and gut-wrenching fear!

As I mentioned earlier, my Diddy chose me to be his favorite. I never quite understood what or why he chose me, but in some ways, I was glad, and in other ways, it made me very sad. You see, being a favorite did have its perks; as I said, I never was the recipient of one of the belt chasings or "child-go-round" whoopings, and I never got things thrown at me, or my toys busted, but I was, I think, the recipient of jealousy from my siblings. My being the favorite and not getting treated by our Diddy like they were, I think, caused them to *need* to be mean to me. Whether it was making me eat bugs—by convincing me that they had also swallowed the bugs in the bottom of the glass bottles that were stored outside—or making me cry and believe that when I started school, I would have to climb over tall walls to go anywhere in school, and snakes and such would be on the other side waiting for me. What I didn't realize at that time was that they were just being mean to me because, in their little minds, I deserved some meanness too… but I truly believed them. I'm sure I would have felt the same as they did 'cause, after all, they didn't deserve what was being done to them either. They also sought some perks from me and would take advantage of my favoritism at times and get me to be the gopher and ask for things… like cookies and the like for all of us. I was always happy to try 'cause, after all, they were my security, and I needed them as much, if not more, as they needed me. I try to remember ever feeling, at this age, that I had a safety net in my parents. I can't honestly say that I felt safe with my Mama or Diddy. They gave me life and a dwelling, but the love, nurturing, and security of knowing they wouldn't allow harm to come to us was something I didn't feel. I want to believe, at this age, that I had at least one parent that I felt I could trust, but if I did (and I honestly cannot remember), the mistrust overruled any sense of trust or normalcy that may have existed. Even though I was never the recipient of the whoopings, the toll it took on my poor little heart and mind was painstakingly overwhelming. The fear and anguish and heartache I felt for my siblings at 212 Robert Avenue is something that I buried deep from childhood. This wasn't discussed by any of us siblings until a few years ago, and this wasn't forgotten. We didn't have a choice… so we all just survived… at "212 Robert Avenue."

212 Robert Avenue

What happened in the walls of this humble abode,
Are parts of the story that you were just told,
Some of the memories I have chosen to leave behind,
But they will forever be etched in the children's little minds,
Because even though we are all now adults,
It caused all this hurt and pain I have shared as a result,
But even though it was hard to understand,
I know it must have been part of the Lord's great plan,
For me to survive and share this story with you,
So, you can see what the Lord can also do,
For He is there in the midst of our pain,
Just waiting for us to call out His name,
And He will be there and come to our rescue,
And give us a life that we never knew,
A life of peace, promise, and gain,
I will be the Lord's vessel and will always proclaim,
That if you surrender yourself to His loving arms,

Then nothing can hurt you, and you will be free from life's
* harm,*
I gave my life to Him in 1992,
Now I can let go of 212 Robert Avenue,
This is part of what He wants me to do!
Amen

Written on August 29, 2015, at 6:54 a.m.

CHAPTER 2
A New Frontier

1966–1970: Fourth Grade Through Seventh Grade

I realize that what we experienced as children molded us all into who we became as adults. I can't speak for all my siblings, or my parents for that matter, but I know that our years at 212 Robert Avenue had an overwhelming impact on all of us. Some of the things that happened I blocked out or may have been too young to remember, but my older siblings remember and have shared more. Things did get better when we moved to a small town outside of metropolitan Atlanta when I was in the fourth grade. But my Diddy was still someone to always be feared as long as I lived there. The fits of rage and whoopings were less frequent and/or memorable, but we all knew how the beast inside could be unleashed at the drop of a hat.

Not sure exactly what may have caused the decline of Diddy's outbursts. I can analyze now and say maybe it was because we moved from the approximately eight hundred square foot dwelling to a larger, maybe twelve hundred square foot dwelling for eight people. This gave my sister (Sis) and me a bedroom to ourselves, a dresser and chest of drawers to ourselves, and our own closet. This also gave my four brothers a room to themselves. Each one of them had their own twin-size stacked bunk bed with one dresser, one drawer for each of them, and a closet for the four of them to share. Mama and Diddy had the master bedroom, which had a small bathroom and only enough room for them to put their full-size bed, dresser, and chest of drawers, and they barely had room to walk around to make the bed. But we had another bathroom in the hallway, which of course, became the kid's bathroom.

We also had a dining room with a table big enough for all of us, a living room, and a very, very small kitchen. Our dwelling at 212 didn't have a table big enough for all eight of us at one time. Later on, the carport was enclosed and made into a den, which gave us an additional room. So all the additional rooms, in my analogy, allowed people to hide or stay out of sight or mind as much as possible. Or could it be that my Diddy wasn't taking those pills anymore? I only remember the pills being an ever-curious presence before we moved.

Did you notice that I have referenced our dwelling above instead of our home? You see… the definition of "home" is "the abiding place of the affections, especially domestic affections;" that is not what we had by any form of the definition. "Dwelling" definition, on the other hand, "abode or residence," is more suitable, in my opinion.

Remember? I said earlier Diddy's outbursts weren't as often; well, that doesn't mean they didn't still exist. Not exactly sure of my age, but it was after the move in fourth grade, which would make me nine or older. One day my Diddy, just out of the blue, to me anyway, threw his cigarette lighter across the living room at my sister (Sis), who was six years older than me, so she had to be at least fourteen or fifteen or so, and hit her in the head with it. It hit so hard that it busted her head open, and I remember him yelling he wished she would have d*** died when my Mama took her to the bathroom to stop the bleeding.

> *My sister has since shared with me that she knew she was bleeding,*
>> *but she was afraid to move until Mama saw the blood trickle down her shirt,*
>> *and she took her to the bathroom.*

This is the only scenario I remember the reason behind my Diddy's behavior, and it was because my Mama had begun working at this time, and I believe it was on a Saturday because we didn't have school, and she must have had to work. We were all in the living room, and my Mama had asked what time we had gotten up that morning, and my Diddy said a certain time, and my sister said another time. Not sure if it was simultaneous or if they disagreed about what she had said as opposed to what he had said or not, but either way, what happened next was unbelievable. Just her saying the time was different was all it took to spark his rage. His rage was so instant and hateful that he even wished death upon my sister out loud. That was a hard thing to witness, understand, or comprehend as a nine-year-old child, which was around the age I probably was. I can't even begin to imagine how my sister of around fourteen felt hearing her Diddy wish death upon her for something as trivial as the time, or a few minutes difference in time, or hours for that matter.

My sister was a beautiful person, inside and out, and I never understood why he chose to be so mean to her. She received the major brunt of his rage, along with the next to the oldest of my brothers. They both have shared things that I don't remember, as I said before, and quite honestly, I'm glad that I don't. Diddy's emotional injustices to my sister included even me in a very negative way. He compared the two of us, out loud. They were unjust and undignified comparisons of two of your very own children. Something so outrageous and crude as even telling her that my butt would make her a Sunday face. What parent, or anyone for that matter, would want to inflict such emotional scars on not only their beautiful child but any child, for that matter? I can't imagine that any of us were bad kids. We weren't allowed to be, not one iota. So much so that the rule in the car was that you sat there with your feet and legs straight in front of you. Not allowed to move. Something as basic as crossing your legs in the car wasn't allowed. No crossing your legs, or you would be in serious trouble, and we all knew what being in trouble with Diddy meant.

Well, now that I have shared a lot of pain, it's time to share some gain that this "new frontier" gave me.

We, kids, had some good times playing games in the yard with the neighbors.

For the first time I can remember in my life, I felt playing outside was not a punishment because I was born, but it was something I chose to do because I liked it. You see, we had lots of neighbors that had kids, and we would get together and play all kinds of awesome outdoor games. Thank goodness there wasn't such a thing as Atari, Nintendo, Wii, Xbox, or any number of the other newest indoor gadgets that kids are inundated with nowadays. We had to use our minds and bodies to have fun, and we always did. From softball, dodgeball, football, Red Rover, Simon Says, Red Light, Green Light, marbles, pick up the sticks, Barrel of Monkeys, stilt walking, and barrel walking to Ante Over, of which the last three were some of my favorites. I was good at walking on stilts and would spend hours walking a fifty-five-gallon drum around the yard 'cause I was very good at that.

Ante Over was probably my favorite game, and many people I tell about Ante Over have never heard of it nor know how to play it, but it was so much fun. Maybe we made it up? Probably need to google it. So, here's how it goes… the instructions.

- You need an A-frame house or building with yard on all sides.
- You pick teams, the more, the merrier.
- Each team will be sent to either front or back of the A-frame yard.
- You take a ball; any ball, if it is soft, big, small, or medium, it doesn't matter.
- The team that has the ball to begin with (however that is decided; coin toss, number guess…) will throw the ball over the house and yell "ante over" as the ball is thrown.

- The team on the other side doesn't know where the ball will come from on the other side, so all eyes have to be on the lookout. Right, left, middle, in the air, or on the roof. Out of bounds is outside of the house boundary on the sides and another boundary that you agree upon for the back boundary. Out of bounds has to throw again.
- The object for the team being thrown the ball is for someone on this team to catch the ball, either in the air or as it comes off the house. It cannot hit the ground.
- If someone catches it, then they can go around the house to the other team's side, they can choose the right side of the house or the left side of the house, but they must be ready to throw the ball at the other team members because when they see them, they will be running to get away and not get hit. If they hit them, they must become their team member and be brought to their side of the house.
- So the object for the team throwing the ball is to try to make it hard for them to catch as well as all eyes watching for either the ball to be "ante over'ed" back, if the other team doesn't catch it, or they have to watch for the other team to come from either side of the house and run in order not to be hit by the ball and become the other team's team member. The sides of the house are the safe zone. Once all team members are safe, if no one gets hit by the ball, the other team has to "ante over."
- The game continues until one team has all players or everyone is too tired to play anymore.

We, kids, learned what a garden was and how much work it took.

We, kids, also learned about other things such as animals, grass cutting, laundry, housekeeping, and cooking.

Boys mostly did the feeding of the animals while the girls shared the gardening.

Girls only did the housekeeping, clothes washing, and cooking.

I enjoyed cutting grass, so I did that, too. My sister and I realized the chores weren't even, but we did our duties without complaining, except to each other.

We, kids, all became worker bees.

The house and land where we moved to had seven acres of land, I think. We had a barn, some horses, pigs, and chickens. We had a clothesline that was double rows and spanned a large distance in the backyard. We had an old washing machine where you had to run the clothes through the rolling pins to ring them out. Imagine doing that for eight people. I'm sure we wore our clothes until they were sure enough dirty and didn't dare change twice in one day.

At first, we had a garden in our backyard that was between the clothesline and the barn. We had corn, okra, squash, tomatoes, cucumbers, watermelons, cantaloupes, green beans, butter beans, purple hull beans, black-eyed peas, potatoes, peanuts, and probably some more stuff. Later my Diddy decided that wasn't enough garden for all of us, so he started renting land. Not sure if he thought it wasn't enough garden to keep all of us kids busy or enough garden to keep us all fed but nonetheless, it wasn't enough for him. He rented across the road, up the road, down the road, in other towns, or wherever he could find land for rent.

One day he even signed us kids up to help another family pick their cotton. We weren't too happy 'bout that 'cause, after all, we hadn't ever picked cotton, and we were done with our gardening that year, and we felt we had done enough gardening. It was back-breaking work too, and I got bit by their dog picking that cotton… for them. I think we got paid, but that didn't matter; it wasn't our cotton. That was what we or I thought, anyway. We only did that one time, so I don't know if it was the dog bite or some other reason that was a one-time thing. Whatever it was, I was glad. Kudos to those for having cotton, but if I had to pick… I'd rather work on all the vegetables we had as opposed to picking cotton. After all, if I got hungry while working, I could take my *pick*, and no one would know anything was missing.

With all the land Diddy rented came endless hours spent in the gardens. "Gardens" is plural because we always had more than one. It seemed to me he couldn't have enough gardens. We, kids, on the other hand, would have been fine with the one in the backyard. From laying out the rows to planting, hoeing, and harvesting, it was an endless daily or weekly chore that we had to do, and we better do it and not be slackers… or else. Several times my sister and I did ours and the boy's chores to keep us all out of trouble because they didn't seem to understand, like we did, that if the boys didn't do their part, we all got in trouble. On second thought, maybe they did and knew that if they slacked, we would make sure it got done to keep everybody out of trouble. I have proudly told many coworkers that I was a hoer growing up, just to see the look on their faces. Shame on them for thinking I was proudly proclaiming to be the other kind… gotta love a sense of humor!

I remember that one of the plots my Diddy rented had the longest, seemingly, never-ending rows.

I was forever looking for the end of the row, but the bad thing was I knew that once I got to the end of that row, I came up another, and so on, and so on, and so on, until it was time for the day to end. I couldn't wait for those days to end. No need to complain or ask to go home because that wouldn't be a good thing to do. So, we went down and up, row after row, after row, after painstaking row. I would guess they had to be a least a mile long each.

I don't see how it would take this much land and rows to feed us. As I said, it was never-ending work. Once the harvest was done, our jobs were endless hours of sitting around the swing in the backyard or in the kitchen, peeling, popping, shucking, slicing, dicing, canning, blanching, and freezing. One thing I can say for sure, we did have some good food to eat. We knew what it took to get it too. I refuse to own a garden now.

I never will forget the time I was walking a fifty-five-gallon drum around in the yard, which was another of my favorite pastimes, and Diddy came out and said it was time to work in the garden. I wasn't finished with my drum walk and was fussed at to come on. In the rush to stay out of trouble, I failed to realize or remember I didn't have shoes on. The dirt gets very hot in the hot sun, and the bottom of my feet were burning with each move to each stalk of corn I had to hoe. Yes, I even remember it was corn only on this trip. I begged to go back across the street to get my shoes, but the answer was no. Therefore, I had to get creative to come up with a way that I could hoe and not hurt my feet at the same time. So, I became a chicken, except for the pecking part. With each move to another stalk, I dug into the dirt with each foot. I was never too busy to realize or remember my shoes again.

I also made some friends along the way during this timeframe that will forever have an impact on my life, and they probably never even knew it.

I think I was in the fifth or sixth grade, and I made friends with Alice and Elaine. To me, they were rich. Not sure if they actually were or if it was only my impression, but I based my fact of their wealth strictly on their home as well as their family. I made friends with Alice first. Alice invited me to go to church with her one day. My experience with church prior to her invitation was a recollection I had that wasn't too pleasant and, quite frankly, scary. You see, I had gone to a small church at some point in my childhood with my parents, for some reason; I'm not sure why or where it was, but I remember what the preacher was doing and some of what he was saying. He was talking about something called "h***," "fire," and the "devil," and someone called "Jesus." The most prevalent thing I remembered him doing, though, was yelling and shaking his head and his finger and stomping. I was afraid that any minute he might grab me and give me a whooping because I didn't know about this "h***," "fire," "a devil," and "a Jesus." I believe that made the impression on me that church was not a fun place and surely not something I ever cared to participate in, ever again in my life. The preacher's anger reminded me too much of my Diddy.

So, when Alice asked me to come, I am positive I turned her down and told her why, and she had to educate me as well as coax me into going with her by telling me how much fun it was and all the things they did. I liked Alice because she was very sweet, so I trusted her and went, even though I had to subdue my fears and hesitation to do so. Well, I attended, and I was somewhat—if not "a lot of what"—intimidated. You see, their Sunday school teacher shared a story and asked questions about it, and my friend Alice knew all the answers. I, on the other hand, didn't have a clue who Nicodemus was or where he hid or why he hid. So, I think I went with her a time or two after that. I was still feeling intimidated and intrigued at the same time but couldn't help but feel like I didn't belong because my friend was very smart about all this Jesus stuff, and it was also apparent to me that it must be a book that taught you lots, cause my friend knew lots. Also, their teaching approach was a lot different than what I had experienced earlier. They taught more about love. The love of Jesus? A man called Jesus that could save me? What was this thing called love all about? Who and where was this man called Jesus that could be my Father? That was something all new and different to me. A Father that loved? Could there possibly be such a thing? A Father that would and could love not only me but lots of others? Were there others like me that needed a new Father? Were there others like me that needed saving? This was all very confusing but interestingly intriguing, nonetheless.

Shortly thereafter, quite ironically, out of the blue, the neighbors two doors up from me began having church in the basement of their home. I asked permission and may have even begged for permission to go. I remember being excited to find out more about this man called "Jesus" and what they actually meant by a "heavenly Father." I must admit I wasn't at all excited to find that He lived in the sky, and I couldn't see Him, or talk to Him, or move in with Him, but all I could do was pray to Him and know that He heard me and loved me and was my Savior.

- I wanted a Father I could see.
- I needed a Father I would see.
- I wanted a Father I could talk to, and He could talk to me.
- I needed a Father I would talk to, and He would talk to me.
- I wanted a Father I could love, and He could love me.
- I needed a Father I would love, and He would love me.
- I wanted a Father who could save me.
- I needed a Father who would save me.
- I decided to be okay with the fact that He was somewhere and would be all these things to and for me, but I still wanted and needed Him to be present with me!
- The church was short-lived in that home and was moved from the home two doors up into town.
- I was discouraged because that meant it wasn't possible for me to go, but I had at least learned that there was an awesome Father somewhere out there!
- I also learned that Father loved me!
- Hence—"A New Frontier."

A New Frontier

Well, hallelujahs for the story that you just heard,
A seed was planted, and I heard the Word,
The problem with this was I wasn't quite ready to give,
But I thought I was just beginning to live,
In this new frontier that had been given to me,
But nonetheless, I knew there was a Father that I wanted to
*   see,*
Along with this new frontier knowledge, I was given a
*   powerful dream,*
And for many years, I wondered—what did it mean?

The Horizon

I was walking down a dirt road and looking down at my feet,
And I couldn't believe who, on that dirt road, I did meet,
My feet were filthy with red dirt from the road,
On each side of me was a child, and their hands I did hold.

As I raised my eyes to look up ahead,
What I saw on the entire horizon was Jesus instead,
Of the sun or the sky or the birds up above,
All I can remember was feeling His powerful love!

He was speaking to me maybe in a way that only He knew,
But now I know He was telling me what He wanted me to
*   do!*
So, you have just heard the story of how this new frontier was
*   given for me to see,*
And during this chapter, the Lord came from the sky to visit
*   with me!*

Even though I was upset to find that He was somewhere in
the sky,
He did come to me in that dream, and I felt His all-powerful
eye,
Watching over me from that day on,
Even though I have faltered, I was never alone!

Now I believe I must share my sorrows and pain,
So that if you listen, you too will see what you can also gain,
By surrendering your heart, mind, body, and soul,
To the Father of all fathers and, oh my, what beauty you will
behold!

The peace, love, and joy that I now feel,
Is something that is so powerful and oh-so real!
I'm so thankful He came to me on that dirt road,
So that this story you have just heard can now be told!

This is the chapter of "A New Frontier"
But lo and behold, life's sorrows don't end here!
Amen

Written on August 29, 2015, at 7:33 a.m.

CHAPTER 3
What Lies Ahead

1971–1974: Eighth Through Twelfth Grade

Now that I have shared what beauty I found in knowing that there is a heavenly Father that is ever present and that He wants to be around. I also heard of someone called Satan, who wanted to seal my fate, to not be with the Father that had visited with me on whatever was that date, but that he wanted me to follow him down a path that, I believe he thought, would lead to the destruction of me!

> *So, from 1970 to 1992, as you will see in the chapters that will follow, the devil had his hold on me and took me places I never wanted to see or be.*

As I entered high school, which was in the eighth grade, at our tiny school, there was something that I thought was what I should be more interested in than books, or learning, or math, or shorthand… but something called a boy that should later be called a man.

Well, I began to look around and see who I might take a liking to, and I also wanted to see who might take a liking to me. There were a few candidates that caught my fancy, and we went steady for a short while. One was a smooth talker with a great smile, but it didn't take much more than a week for me to figure out he was playing trick or treat! That was my version of what is now called a player.

Then, in homeroom, there was a seemingly shy and mysterious boy that caught my eye. He was very handsome with big dark eyes that seemed to see into your soul with just a glance, and so I began to try to start up something called a romance. He seemed very aloof even though I had tried for a few weeks just to get him to notice me, so I finally decided one day that I would begin to look another way. So, I didn't go to the same room I had been going to during break because I decided it wasn't meant to be; after all, he hadn't even noticed me. So, I went to another room instead and found someone else who was also very handsome, with big dark eyes, but had very gentle and kind eyes. He noticed and even talked to me! So, needless to say, I was smitten quite a bit because only one day had elapsed, and we had a conversation, and he also smiled as he looked at me.

Well, that evening, I received a phone call. The boy on the other end told me at first that he was the one I had the conversation with. Soon into the conversation, he confessed he was the boy, who had, for many weeks, pretended not to notice me. I wondered how he knew that I had gone to another room and actually talked to another boy, and he even knew his name… because, after all, he wasn't there. His brother was in the same room and had told him where I went and who I had talked to. I was somewhat confused because I had begun to really like the way the other boy looked at me, smiled at me, and talked to me, but nonetheless, he had, after all, been the one I had my eye on, **or so I thought**, for several weeks so I decided to see where this conversation would lead. We began to talk on the phone and flirt with each other at school, but it wasn't long before I was hearing and being told things of which I had never heard. I don't recall how long it was before the things that this boy wanted to teach me were whispered in my ear on the telephone. Words, as I said, I had never heard before, and I remember thinking as he was telling these things to me, *How does he know all this stuff? Because it sure isn't taught in school.* He knew words and the meanings of such things I had never heard of, and he questioned me as to whether I liked this stuff. I didn't want to seem dumb, but I had to admit that I wasn't sure what either of them meant, but maybe I would like it… wasn't quite sure. Well, he made sure that I was taught about this and much, much more because he gave and assigned me some reading material. He gave me two books and instructed me to be sure and read both. One was *The Sensuous Man*, and the other was *The Sensuous Woman*.

First, I wondered and questioned how and where someone of our young age could be so knowledgeable as well as have these kinds of books at his age… never saw these kinds of books at school. Well, he proudly proclaimed that he had ordered them when he was twelve, and they were sent to his home. I wondered how someone of our age would have the money or the knowledge to find out how to get books like this through the mail… or why they would. He explained that he had ordered them, but because he was underage that they didn't have to be paid for… they couldn't make him pay for them. I'm sure when I analyze this now; there must have been many denials that no one there had ordered or received such books. So, Mom or Dad had probably refused the invoices and called the place that sent them and advised they were never received or requested by anyone at this residence. Nonetheless, instead of seeing all the signs that I now know were screaming out at me that this was a road I shouldn't take… the books I was assigned to read talked about love and intimacy… which were two things I had yearned for since childhood. So, I'm sure I decided to just read the books and learn my assignment in hopes of finding someone to love me. I wasn't ready for the intimacy that was described in these books; I just wanted someone to be intimate with me by spending time with me, laughing with me, flirting with me, and just being my boyfriend. A boy who wanted to talk to me and kiss me and do things to me that were described in these books was overwhelming and intimidating to me, to say the least, so I would discuss things with him but never do these things… for some time.

I was able to forgo this intimacy that I had learned about in my book assignments until he was able to drive a car. So, looking back, even though these books were given to me in the eighth grade, it wasn't until two years later that he got to do to me what he had planned for a couple of years. Don't get me wrong; I am not blaming him for my actions. I could have, and should have, not done anything until I was ready and wanted to experience this part of life, but instead, I succumbed to his wishes as well as his pressure to give in. I knew it was wrong, and I also knew that if my Diddy found out about this that he would kill me... and or him.

You see, my Diddy had decided early on, the first time he saw this boy, that he didn't like him and forbade me to see him. My Diddy didn't even have a conversation with him. He just looked at him and decided that he was a "d***" hippie. I couldn't understand how my Diddy could instantly decide that he didn't like someone and that I was not allowed to talk to him or be his girlfriend because he was a "d***" hippie. He had jet-black hair that was shoulder-length but did not go down his back, which was my version of a hippie. He rode his Yamaha 650 motorcycle, which he explained he had financed and was buying and driving, which I didn't understand at fifteen years old, which also probably made my Diddy decide he was a hippie. I, on the other hand, was excited about the motorcycle. I, after all, had ridden dirt bikes in the yard and dune buggies in the yard. So, to me, this was an exciting, adventurous road vehicle, and I couldn't wait to be able to ride it. I was, however, restricted from not only riding the motorcycle but from having anything to do with this "d***" hippie who had shown up at my dwelling as my boyfriend. It didn't go over well at all.

Well, as most of us know, when you as a young adult are forbidden, most of the time, it makes it more important for you to do what you have been forbidden to do. So, I continued my journey down this road and secretly saw him. My friends would come and pick me up and take me to him. We would, of course, have to tell fibs, but that was just a price I had to pay to be able to see him. It wasn't until one night my parents went to a singing out of town that my fibs caught up with me.

He had come over on his motorcycle, and I decided if I was ever going to get to ride, the time was now. He wasn't prepared to take a rider and only had one helmet. We argued over who should wear it. He wanted me to, and I said he should since he was on the front and if we ran into cops, then he would need it. Not sure why he insisted I wear it, but if I hadn't been the one to wear it, I might not be here today. You see, we began the trip on Highway 78, to Tom Brewer Road, and crossed over Highway 81 onto my friends Elaine and Alice's Road. I remember going across and remember him going kinda fast, and then I remember him looking back at something down the road behind us. That is the last thing I remember until I was being shaken and my name was yelled out. You see, when he looked back, which I later found out that he was looking back to see if his friends he had seen at the corner store were following, we went into a curve, and he lost control when the motorcycle came off the road. I was thrown off the motorcycle, hitting the pavement with both my head and my left thigh and was knocked unconscious and ended up in a garden, of all things, and was lost in a bean patch. He was unable to find me for a while as it was just getting dark outside. He was screaming and yelling for me, but since I was unconscious, I was unable to respond. When I came to and realized what had happened and realized I had dirt and mud all in my mouth, I remember thinking I didn't want him to see me looking like this. I was spitting out dirt. How unattractive! *I don't want him seeing me like this*, is all I was thinking. It wasn't until I came to my senses that I realized what I should and needed to be concerned about. My Diddy! Oh my, what was I going to do? How was I going to be able to fib my way out of this? Fortunately, my head was okay, but unfortunately, my left thigh was all scraped up, and I would not be able to hide it or the pain. His parents took me to the hospital, but since they were not my parents, and there was no such thing as pagers or cell phones back then, I had the painstaking wait… wait until they got home from the concert… and I had to tell them and show them what had happened.

Of course, you can probably guess my Diddy's reaction. Yes, he was very mad at me, but he said he was going to kill my boyfriend. To this day, I'm not sure how that didn't happen, but from this day forward, it made it harder for him and me to continue to be boyfriend and girlfriend, going steady as our classmates called us from age fourteen to seventeen, when *I* graduated. Notice the "I." Yep, he quit school. He got in trouble for being late all the time or just not showing up for school, so he had too many tardies and absences to graduate. Besides, he always seemed to be in trouble with the principal.

But with friends, we managed to continue our "steady-ship" or courtship as it was called back then all the way through to twelfth grade without any more wrecks or incidences where we got caught. All was going well, or so it seemed, and I was crowned as the Homecoming Queen, and He and I were chosen as The Cutest for Senior Superlatives. We did, however, have a breakup in twelfth grade, just before I graduated. You see, I somehow found out that my boyfriend was doing something that I highly unapproved of. I found out that he was smoking marijuana. I don't remember how I found out, but I do remember telling him that if he was doing stuff like that, I didn't want to be his girlfriend anymore, and we broke up. No more going steady for us. He, however, begged and convinced me that he would not do it anymore if I didn't want him to and that he wanted to be my boyfriend and would give that up and not ever, not never, do it again… for me. I, of course, believed him, and we went steady again, boyfriend and girlfriend!

… and on December 21, 1974, we were married.

Puppy Love

Puppy love is called that for more than one reason,
It is called that because it only lasts for a season,
Puppies may grow up and become hard to handle,
To get a good dog, it is kind of a gamble!

They can be good, but you will not know,
Until you take them home and let them grow,
They can be obedient and good,
But you want to know if you really want them, or if you should!

Until you take them home to be part of your life,
And if they will cause happiness, joy, or strife,
If they gnaw up everything and won't leave well enough alone,
And you wish you could find them a new home!

But you try to train them and teach them instead,
Or spank them with newspaper and send them to bed,
But no matter how hard with some of them you try,
The initial joy that you felt may have been just a lie,
Sometimes you cannot teach a dog a new trick!
And you feel with each turn that you are the one getting licked!

But you still try your best with each passing day,
Until you are exhausted and must find another way!
But you remember the joy and love that you felt in your heart,
When you first laid eyes upon it, you knew you would never part!

So, take what lessons from this can be learned,
Be true to yourself and answer your hearts yearn!
To be happy and joyful in this short life,
And be free from a whole lot of strife,
Whether it is a puppy or a human to love,
Make sure it is a gift that is sent from up above!
Amen

Written on September 8, 2015, on my fifty-ninth birthday

CHAPTER 4

Deception Abound

1975–1990: Ages Eighteen Through Thirty-Four

I did find the nerve to ask my Diddy if we could get married before we did it and his response was, "H*** no"! So, because I thought I was in love, and I thought he also loved me, and I thought everything would be wonderful if we could just be together, I planned and paid for our entire wedding. I worked at Hartford Insurance Company in Atlanta as a shorthand transcriber. I carpooled with a gentleman from town and several other ladies every day on this long trip from our small town into Atlanta.

I saved my money, and we decided to marry one Saturday when my Diddy would be gone on a trip as a truck driver. I'm sure, even then, I may have thought it might be best if he didn't make it home. I told my Mama I was doing it, and she, of course, knew that it was happening but also knew there was nothing she could do to stop it. Short of telling my Diddy before it happened, and he got a gun after one or both of us. I think back and wish that she didn't have to be the one to tell my Diddy where I was when he came home. You see, 'cause I had seen my Diddy get mean to my Mama too and hit her. My two oldest brothers got mad and went on a search for him. They were old enough by this time to band together and not take the abuse anymore. Not exactly sure what happened, but I don't think they found him. But they took me to school and let me know what they were doing and why they wouldn't be at school. I was glad 'cause I didn't like seeing my Mama get hit either, but I was also scared for my brothers.

Anyway, neither of my parents attended my wedding. My next to the oldest brother gave me away. Sad that I had to ask him to do that and that I didn't think of what trouble I may be getting him into for giving me away. But by this time, he was twenty, and I don't recall if he was living at home or not. Nevertheless, I guess my Diddy just figured since I had done this even though he had said, "H*** no," that it was done...

... and I would have to live with my decision.

Live with my decision, I did for twenty-three years. Was it good, was it great, was it wonderful, and was it the best decision in my life? Not by a long shot.

Trouble began as soon as we were married. You see, I told you earlier that I paid for the entire wedding; well, on our honeymoon I found out that he had to borrow not only a car for it but also the money for it as well. I didn't understand that because he also worked and lived at home just like I did, so I questioned him why he had to borrow money. I don't remember his excuse, but in my eyes, it had to be an excuse because, in my eyes, there was no excuse. Well, not long after that, I found out part of the reason money had to be borrowed. A lot of his money went to buy—yep, you guessed it—marijuana.

You see, I would go to work at the grocery store in town because he had convinced me to quit my job in Atlanta because I was gone too much. He was supposed to pick me up—I still didn't drive, that is how reserved and afraid of the world I was—but he wouldn't show up to get me when I got off. This happened quite often, and I had no one to call to come to get me and take me home but my Mama. Mama would ask me what was going on when we got to my house, and there were cars everywhere, and I would tell her I didn't know. I'm sure she would tell Diddy 'bout this, and that probably explains why even though he had to accept the fact that we were married, it didn't change the fact that he had to talk to him or acknowledge him, which he didn't for eight years! Well, anyway, I would get to our house, and there would be all kinds of people at my house. Yep, you guessed it, smoking marijuana and having a great time partying at my house while I didn't have a ride home because my husband had forgotten me. I would just come in and go to our bedroom and sit and wait for the party to end.

Well, it didn't end… but it was the beginning of my husband begging me to partake in this part of his life… that he wanted to be part of our lives. We had many arguments and breakups over this. I can remember being so upset that I told him to pull the car over and let me out. He wouldn't do it until I made him understand that I was getting out whether he stopped or not, so he did. This went on for about six months, I would say, until he finally got his way. He had begged and pleaded and told me how awesome it was and how wonderful I would feel. I had stood my ground with all his other pleas to try it, but one day I finally caved in.

If we were going to be together, this was the only way it was going to work because we had done nothing but fight and separate over it. We had even lost our house because of it. So, here we go on our merry way from a nice mobile home we had gotten from my sister and brother-in-law, and because we broke up and had so much trouble, we ended up letting them have it back and then moved to an old farmhouse that was more than a hundred years old and was way off the road behind the owner's home on a whole lot of farmlands. Well, my husband loved it, and I wasn't too happy about it! You see, it had four bedrooms, a living room, a kitchen, and an entryway with a bathroom at the end. The bathroom floor was so weak and in need of repair that you could feel the floor give way when you walked in. And it wasn't very pretty either! There was nothing pretty at all about it. The rooms were big with high ceilings, and the windows were not weather-resistant. It was so cold in the winter we had to eventually move into the living room only because we ran out of gas so quickly, just trying to live in one half of the house. We tried living in the kitchen, our bedroom, the living room, and the entryway with the bathroom, but the gas only lasted for a little while like that, and we couldn't afford it. The other three bedrooms were on the other side of the house, and that part became his garage. Motorcycles torn apart, tools everywhere, and party central became the rest of the house, unless it was in the living room. The kitchen was very big and only contained a sink cabinet. The sinks were so worn they wouldn't come clean. One night there was a rat in the kitchen, not a mouse, mind you, but a wolf rat. My husband threw a wrench at it and killed it. That was fun to him, but I hated the fact that there could be, and there was, a creature like that in my house with me!

Needless to say, I was not a happy camper at this place. It was not my picture of the wonderful life I had planned. But me being me, I made the best of it, and I decorated and painted to make it better. We were so poor that our living room chairs were outdoor furniture. They were wood, though, and big, so it worked to fill space, and I made myself believe it was kinda neat. I really didn't feel I had a choice, so they were kinda neat. I realized they weren't so neat when my sister and her husband visited, and I saw the puzzled look on their faces and their questions about why we had lawn furniture in the living room as chairs. His mom gave us a couch, which was gold and cream flowered. So, here we are in our old farmhouse, living uncomfortably and having fun! My husband had taken advantage of the fact that we were living on a farm, and he planted and began to grow his own marijuana, and he was very proud. He was too proud and showed it to too many people, I guess, so at harvest time, the stalks mysteriously disappeared.

I found that his pride, his marijuana, had been taken right out from under him after I left.

Here's where this story gets even crazier. I have a hard time remembering exactly how long we had been married before the, to me, unthinkable happened. I think it had been between a year and a half to two years (a year in the mobile home and maybe a year in the farmhouse) when my husband—who I snuck around to see and had to fib to my Diddy and Mama about, allowed him to do things to me before I was even ready to understand them, married and paid for our wedding, surrendered to his begging and pleas to try marijuana—suddenly, and out of the blue asked me for a "five-year legal separation."

As he explained, he wanted a five-year legal separation from me, and then we would get back together, and I would have his children. I was the woman he wanted to have his children, but he wanted and needed this separation from me because he needed variety and wanted to be with other women! We were fourteen when we started going steady, had married at eighteen, and then we were twenty when he suddenly decided he needed to be with other women for "five years"!

Oh, and he also told me that if I knew how ugly my stretch marks were that I would get rid of them. You see, I have a few scars from a surgery I had when I was fourteen. I had a cyst on the end of my spine. It was so huge they had to cut a big hole about two inches deep and two inches wide. They left it open, and it had to close by itself. Had I known that this would cause my skin to stretch, I could have lubricated and possibly prevented the marks. Unfortunately, though, they must have been so grotesque to my husband that he wanted to be with other women; after all, why else would he tell me and especially at the same time he asked for the "five-year legal separation." After all I had been through and had given into to make him happy, I remember feeling devastated.

Well, needless to say, I wanted no part of a "five-year legal separation" and immediately told him he was nuts. I told him that we would get a divorce, but a separation was out of the question and, quite frankly, the craziest thing I had ever heard, and besides that, there was no such thing. Not to my knowledge anyway, but he assured me there was. Guess he had ordered a book on that too. So, in order to leave him, I had to get my license because I still didn't drive. I had to get past that fear I had as a child. I remember feeling while riding down the road in our family car and inquiring as to how in the world you could keep a car between the two lines you had to keep it between. I remember thinking and saying that I would never be able to do that! I think my friend, Elaine, took me to get my license the next day, and I never will forget the pride I felt in doing that. I had overcome that childhood fear, and now I was a driver... at twenty!

After getting my license, I decided I would go into Covington and find myself a cute outfit to wear to the house to gather my belongings. I, after all, had decided that once he saw me again, especially if I was wearing a cute new outfit, he would realize how insane his request as well as his thoughts were, and say, "Never mind." So, I showed up adorned in a very form-fitting pair of jeans with red piping and a red and white tube top. I was too cute to turn away... or so I had envisioned. Well, he not only watched me walk away, but he helped me load my belongings and watched me as I drove away. Not sure where my thoughts were at this time, but I can analyze them now and know where they should have been. They should have been full of joy and relief. After all, I was being let go from a life of trials, struggles, temptations, arguing, and by no means living the wonderful life I had planned.

Even though I was crushed, I set out to make myself a new plan... a "me" plan! I visited my Mama and told her I was leaving Georgia because of what had happened because it would be too hard for me to stay around and watch or know of his endeavors knowing what his plans were for my future... in five years! How foolish to think that he could just demand such an endeavor for himself and expecting for me to be there with open arms at the end of his five years. I don't suppose that his mind could conceive the possibility that I just might find someone else to be happy with within his five-year timeframe. Oh, but wait, I suppose in his book of five-year legal separations, that wouldn't happen! Hence, separation, not divorce; therefore, neither he nor I would find someone to replace the one we were destined to be with... in five years!

Crazy, huh?

So, my friend Elaine, who I mentioned earlier, offered me a place to live with some family members of hers that I had met on a week-long camping vacation to Florida, where I had gone with her and her family when I was fifteen. I even remember him trying to make me feel bad about going and trying to convince me not to go because I would be away from him for, oh my gosh, a whole week. As Elaine explained, she had told her family what had happened to me, and they wanted to offer me a place in their home. I turned down the offer because they had three children, and each had a room. They were offering to move their son out of his room and give it to me. They would move him to the living room. I graciously accepted and drove to Florida with another of my friends. My friend, Neece, was so sweet to offer to ride with me there, and the plans were for her to fly back. I never thought of how or where the money came from for her to fly back... but now I wonder. I'm sure we discussed it then, but now I realize how both my friends and my friend's family had sacrificed for me!

That right there was love!
Love in the most innocent and precious and giving of
ways!

Well, I went to Florida, and upon our arrival, my friend and I decided to have a little fun before she flew home, and we went out to eat and dance. I was dancing the pain away and having a good time by myself or with my friend on the dance floor. There was a young gentleman that asked me to dance with him, and I was flattered. I went to the bathroom later, and an older gentleman stopped me and told me I was the prettiest girl there and asked why I was dancing with who I was dancing with. I don't remember what my answer was, but I remember thinking, *I'm the prettiest girl here?* I didn't feel pretty anymore! Not after I had been thrown away as I had. That is exactly what I felt like; someone had just thrown me away, but not just someone... my husband!

I look back at my pictures now, and I was pretty. Not only pretty on the outside but on the inside as well. But, in the turmoil that I was living in, I wasn't pretty or happy. So many pictures he took of me show the hurt and pain in my being. Not only before our "five-year legal separation" episode but also in many episodes that followed.

You see, I wrote his mother to let her know I was okay, and she gave him the letter, and he found me. Yep, you guessed it. I'm sorry, I don't know what I was thinking or why.

"I love you and only you and always will, and God gave me a sign to come and get you." *What? God gave him a sign?* I had never heard him speak of or mention God before. I don't remember his entire story, but supposedly, he had prayed, and God gave him a sign that he was supposed to be with me, and he had to get me back. He called.

I was strong! I didn't want to come back! I had been looking for a job! I had found another way! I was excited about what I had done! After all, I had gotten my license, found myself a place to move to be away from him, and was well on my way to being okay!

But I forgave, and I surrendered again to his pleas, his begging, and his proclamation of his eternal love for me!

Well, we got back together and moved back to the not-so-wonderful farmhouse where this heartache had begun.

And to think that at one point in my life, I felt I couldn't *live* without my boyfriend. Yes, I was confused about my Diddy and the fact that he forbade me to see or talk to him, and I decided at about sixteen that life would just be easier if I didn't have one. I thought it was just too hard to continue the fibs and the forbidding that I decided one day that everyone would be better off if I took some pills and ended my life. Therefore, there would be no Diddy being mad, no boyfriend being hurt that we weren't allowed to see or even talk to one another, and "no me" being in turmoil over it all. I took a bottle full of pills and actually told my boyfriend that I had, and he somehow got in touch with my brother, the one that gave me away. So, I was taken to the hospital, and my stomach was pumped. I remember the fluid was pink. I had eaten some pink sugar wafers before I took the pills. Of all things, I ate some pink sugar wafers with my grandkids today, and this memory was relived with the first bite of the first sugar wafer. It always is!

Well, Diddy must have seen what his behavior was causing because he actually talked to me. He had a real live conversation with me, not just a "demandsation." (My made-up word.) However short the conversation was, it was still a conversation… wow, progress! All he said to me when he found out was to tell me that Mama was worried and that it better not ever happen again. But one would think that when a child is screaming out how unhappy they are with their life or lifestyle, a parent would want to reach out and hug them, or cry with them, or especially tell them that they were loved. But all I got was that Mama was worried. I look back on this now and can't imagine how I could have decided that taking my own life would be the answer to my problem. My problem wasn't worth taking my life… it just felt like it was the only way out of it at the time.

Anyway, as I said, we moved back to the farmhouse. Although I forgave him for his foolishness, I never forgot. I never forgot the hurt, pain, heartache, and the loss of my self-esteem that he had inflicted on me. Although I tried, I never felt the same about our relationship. But

I was old school and believed that once you marry, you do everything in your power to make it work. So, for twenty-two more years… work, I did.

> *Since I could drive now, I was able to take our only car and look for a job while he was at work, and then I would pick him up after he got off.*
> *And I never forgot to go get him.*
> *Later on, I will tell you something else that happened at this time.*

There were so many situations that my book could become way too long, so I will just try to highlight some of the nonsense that our twenty-three-year marriage endured without going into the entire story.

We moved from our hometown area farther south to another small town because my husband was offered a position starting up a new plastic plant. I went to work for a man that lived in the town and owned an exterminating business close to Atlanta. He had a business in the small town we lived in also, which his three boys ran. This man probably was in his mid-fifties and was very kind to me. I had an accident one day on the way home and totaled my car. This man I worked for offered me a car of his to drive until I could get another. I wasn't used to someone being so kind. Well, it wasn't too long before I found out that he wasn't as kind as his gesture of offering me a car to drive. He definitely had an ulterior motive. I was his office manager and did the payroll, accounts payable, and banking information. One day he was opening a new exterminating business and asked me if I would go with him to pick out the curtains for the new office. I didn't think anything about it and said I would go. As we began to drive down the road, he told me that he had a proposition for me. He told me that he wanted me to be his lover! He also told me that if I would, he would supply me with a Corvette Stingray! What? Crazy, huh?

Well, I was devastated and began to cry and apologize to him if I had done anything to make him think I was that kind of person. I assured him that I was not, and I kindly explained to him that I loved my husband, and he was my childhood sweetheart, and I not only would not be able to do what he wanted, but I most definitely would not… not even for a Corvette Stingray, which of course was probably every young girl's dream car.

What made the strongest impact on me was, or the saddest thing to me now, the fact this man portrayed himself as a Christian. He went to church on Sundays with his beautiful, sweet wife, whom I had met. He also had three grown boys my age. And honestly, the impact this had on me caused me to consider myself, who was not a church-goer, as someone who didn't need to go to church if that was what people that went to church did!

I needed a job and couldn't afford to just quit, so I tried to continue to work for him because I was sure he understood where I stood. I tried to do all my bookkeeping work when he was away because all of this was kept in his office, and I definitely didn't want to be caught in his office alone with him. One day not long afterward, he came in while I was working and made it so I couldn't get by him. Somehow, I did, but he did it again in the front office. I don't remember why or what happened, but I had to ride home with him one day, and he insisted I give him a kiss before I got out of the car. He told me he would just be a father figure for me instead. I don't know what kind of father figure he thought he was portraying by wanting to kiss me in the mouth, but I knew my father had never done that, and besides, I was in shock that he even insinuated such a thing after all that he had already done. It was apparent to me that he didn't want to take no for an answer and made it so uncomfortable for me that I had to quit. One day I was there, and the next, I wasn't. My husband wrote him a letter and hand-delivered it to him. I don't remember what it said, but I do remember it was written to make him see how utterly ridiculous he had been. Not sure if it impacted him as there was a new older lady that began working just before I left, and I could see him making moves on her too.

I became pregnant with our first child probably four years into our marriage. I was about four months along and was outside washing and cleaning our new car, and he was sitting on the porch watching. We had purchased a brand-new Z28 Chevrolet Camaro, which replaced the 1964 Chevy pickup I had been driving to work close to Six Flags, which was about a forty-minute drive. I had kindly asked him if he would help me wash it. He turned me down and said he was going to see one of his friends and help him work on a car. He left, and I finished the car alone.

He returned late that night with the news that while he was helping his friend, he found some pictures of me on top of his friend's kitchen cabinets. The pictures of me had to be pictures that his friend took from us when we opened up our home to him for a few weeks because he found his wife was cheating on him, and he was trying to figure out what he wanted to do about it. I was very upset that he had taken the pictures that belonged to us that were only of me and that my husband had taken, and my husband found them at his house while he chose to go help him instead of me. How ironic was that? I didn't consider him much of a friend… but my husband never confronted him.

The next day I began to bleed and actually had a miscarriage and lost the baby. I was somewhat saddened and somewhat relieved at the same time. To me, the behaviors my husband had displayed let me know that he was neither ready to be a father nor the husband to me that I wanted him to be to bring a child into the picture.

A year or so or maybe a few years later, he insisted we stop by to see his friend as he explained he had moved away, and he was now back. They got so stoned, on what I'm not sure, that my husband passed out, and I wasn't able to wake him no matter how hard I tried. His friend insisted I sleep in his bedroom. I didn't want to, but I couldn't get my husband to wake up, and he kept insisting that he wouldn't allow me to sleep in a chair or crammed on the couch with my husband, so I felt I had no choice, and after all, my husband was there. Even though my husband was there, I still felt uneasy knowing what he had done. I was awakened in the night feeling something on my leg, which I believed to be a hand, and he was on the side of the bed on the floor. I asked him what he was doing, and he made up some excuse about looking for something. Needless to say, I was unable to go back to sleep. I told my husband what had happened the next day, when he was coherent, and that I never wanted to be around him again. I never saw him again, but my husband did, and I never did understand that!

A few years later, we moved to South Carolina, where my husband was offered another promotion with another new plastic plant startup. I was twenty-seven going on twenty-eight at this time and felt if we were ever going to be ready, the time was then. I got pregnant and was excited about what the future may hold. That was a short-lived excitement. My husband, on the other hand, didn't seem too excited about the prospect of a baby. Instead of showing excitement, he used some of the changes pregnancy caused to downgrade me and my looks. I was gestational diabetic as well as had a hereditary inflammation called eczema. I kept telling him something was wrong and I needed to see a dermatologist, but he assured me I just needed to quit picking… no matter how much I told him I wasn't picking. The eczema flare-up was on my chin. So here I was, six months pregnant, far away from all family, being fussed at by my husband about my inflammation… that I was causing and feeling pretty sad about the entire situation. Nevertheless, I was a good little stay-at-home wife. I did everything for him, including laying out his work clothes.

One day he was on the front porch working on his motorcycle and suddenly came into the house, all stressed out, telling me he was going to be late for an interview he had to do. I assured him to just jump in the shower, and I would have his clothes all prepared for him so he could make the 1:00 p.m. Saturday interview appointment. Well, he left for the interview, and I didn't see nor hear from him until around 5 a.m. the next morning. Still, to this day, I don't know where he was or what he was doing, but I was devastated. I was hurt that he thought no more of me or our baby to do that, and, after all, I had laid his clothes out for him to go. One of the things I told him many times, as this was not the first time he just disappeared without notice or cause, was happiness was only ten cents away. There were no cell phones or text or pagers or beepers, only house phones, and it would only cost him ten cents to let me know he was okay.

So, I had had enough, and I decided that neither our unborn child nor I was going to live like this. I went to a dermatologist that day to find out what was causing the rash on my chin. I let him know that I had gone and that I was also leaving on a plane that day and flying to Virginia to live with my sister and have the baby there. I was there for about a month and decided I needed to move back to Georgia because I had talked to the company I had worked for before we moved to South Carolina, and they were willing to hire me back and pay me for maternity leave to have the baby. So, as hard as it was, I called my parents. I moved in with them, and my Diddy helped me and actually cosigned for me to get a car that was safe to drive an hour each way to work and back. We had lost the Camaro we had bought earlier because we were unable to make the payments, even though they were around $240 per month. Looking back, I know wages were low then, but a $240 car payment shouldn't have been that hard to manage with two people working full-time and having no kids. We had moved into a cute little log cabin, and the rent was $500 a month, but we still should have been able to do that. Hmmm!

Well, as I said, I moved back to Georgia and in with my parents and began traveling about an hour to work every day, being seven months pregnant.

I began to hear from my husband, and again he pleaded for us to work things out. No woman wants to bring a baby into the world alone and without the father, if possible, so I took a trip to South Carolina, in my ninth month, to discuss things with him. Well, he promised that everything would be different and, of course, I gave in... again! He even found us a nicer and bigger house and moved and even set up everything and prepared for the homecoming.

But some of our old problems reared their ugly head the day I went to the hospital to have the baby. Upon first seeing my husband when he made it to the hospital, I could tell he was seriously stoned, along with his brother, and so could my parents and everyone that was there. I was so embarrassed and disappointed, but nevertheless, I had already broken the news to everyone that we had worked things out, and I would be returning to South Carolina with him and our new-born baby girl... as she turned out to be. You see, I never found out what any of my babies were prior to their birth. I wanted to find out the surprise the Lord had in store as it happened. So, return to South Carolina, I did.

Sure enough, one month after our precious baby girl was born... guess what... another all-night trip away from home... with no ten-cent call... again! He supposedly was going to the races with a friend. Ironically his friend was also married and had a week-old baby, and she and the baby were staying at my house until they returned, which turned out to be the entire night. Our husbands were missing... to us! Surely, we thought, they wouldn't be doing this on purpose after all that we had already been through. Well, at 5 or 6 a.m. the next morning, they both showed up alive and well. I don't recall their excuse or if I even cared to hear it. It didn't matter anymore... it was what it was, and he knew it... so I just had to live with my decision... again!

When someone you have put your trust in this many times continues to misrepresent and abuse the situation, it is disheartening, to say the least. Especially after you have been through all the hurts I had experienced from an early age. But nevertheless, I surrendered to the choices I had made; even though I wasn't happy about it, I still tried to make the best of a not-so-good situation. I was a stay-at-home mom... for the first two years. I went to work and then, a year and a half later, got pregnant again, and he immediately wanted me to quit and stay at home again. So, three and a half years after our first little girl, I gave birth to a wonderfully healthy nine-pound-eleven-ounce baby boy! Again, I was gestational diabetic, but the doctors had no idea he was that big.

Well, during the time of our firstborn and our second, my husband had taken up tennis. He ate, lived, and breathed tennis when he wasn't working. He would come home from work and dress for tennis and return at ten, eleven, or twelve at night... every night and most all weekend too! I was still a stay-at-home mom, his preference, and I began to express how much the kids and I needed some of his spare time to be spent with us. All I did all day, every day, was stay at home, as we only had one car, with the babies. I needed an adult to have a conversation with sometimes, and the kids needed to know and spend time with their father. No matter how I tried to get this across to him, it didn't work.

I was at the end of my rope and decided I would have a discussion with our four-year-old daughter at the time. I asked her what she would think if we—her, her baby brother, and me—didn't live with Daddy anymore. Her response was devastating. This four-year-old little girl responded to me, "That will be okay because he is just a huge monster." First of all, I didn't know she even knew the word huge, but second of all, her four-year-old statement spoke volumes to me! I asked her again what she had said because, as I said, I didn't know she knew the word huge. She, again, reiterated that he was a huge monster.

Hearing that come from her broke my heart. I, too, as a child, had lived with a huge monster; but on the other hand, I was not as poignant as my very own precious four-year-old daughter. I knew where her thoughts probably came from, as he was very bad about yelling and looking very mean if she was playing and even so much as walked in front of the TV. He would yell, "Move out of the way of the TV." I remember trying to tell him that was no way to approach that and that she was just a child. Back then, there were console TVs that sat on the floor, and there was no way not to walk in front of it, but it didn't matter to him. I tried to explain to him that she was more important than the TV. Nothing worked.

The last thing in this world I would want to do is raise a child who envisioned her father to be a monster. So, I decided to meet him at a hotel restaurant to share our daughter's thoughts about him, with him. I just knew that if anything would turn the light bulb on for him that her statement would be it. I chose to meet him at the hotel restaurant in order to alleviate his anger that I thought would be the result, as it usually was if we disagreed about something or the word "divorce" was mentioned. I very calmly, practically, and methodically shared with him the conversation I had with my daughter. It didn't touch him the way I thought it would, but we were able to have a peaceful conversation, and I shared our hurt, our needs, our desires, and our goals for the future, if we were to have one. I expressed I needed more quality time with him, and so did the kids. I felt sure I had made my wishes and desires known, and he would surely not come home and get ready for tennis the next day after work… wrong!

So, I had to either live with my decision or choose to pick up and leave with our two children… and no job. So, I lived with my decision again, and he also lived with his. His life revolved around work and tennis. My life revolved around the home and the children. From the outside looking in, we were the perfect couple. Beautiful parents, beautiful children, a home, a car, a dog… a mere description of what picture-perfect should be. But nevertheless… we fit the picture.

It seems our marriage took on the life of one of those mile-long rows of the garden I had to hoe as a child. Once one row, or one problem, was defeated, there always seemed to be another one just ahead. Some rows or problems were more arduous than the others but always never-ending. Same as the rows in the garden, once one was done, there was always another that needed weeding. Once the weeds were hoed out, they came back and had to be hoed again so the life that was growing could flourish instead of being smothered out by the weeds and not meet its full potential.

Not the Destiny I Would Have Chosen

There once was a poem that was written for me,
It was from my boyfriend about our destiny!
If I had known then what I know now,
I would have chosen a different destiny somehow!

Because all the sorrow, heartache, and pain,
Was not what I set out, in the relationship, to gain!
If I could have seen where this road would lead,
I would have chosen a different route, indeed!

But the road that I took, I cannot change,
I can still grow from this endeavor and call out His name!
And ask for the love that I was searching for,
Even though it wasn't on this road, He still stood at the door!

Waiting for me to call out His name,
And He is there for me, as I hang my head in shame!
Because the choices I made then are choices I now dread,
To share with you because of the thoughts it may put in your
head!

Thoughts of, oh my gosh, I cannot believe,
The choices she made; I cannot conceive!
But please don't think less of me than before,
Because Jesus doesn't, and He looks at me and adores!

As He knows my heart of hearts and that I am this person no
  more,
And as the Bible promises, He's got a lot in store,
For you and me, as we call Him by name!
He will bless us all more than money, gifts, or fame!
He is the healer of all our aches and pain,
I am so glad that I know Him by name!!!
Amen!

Written on September 8, 2015
Written on my fifty-ninth birthday to praise his Holy Name!

CHAPTER 5

A Journey in Search of My Horizon

1991–1992: Ages Thirty-Five and Thirty-Six

My husband had been hired to start up another plastic plant. As part of the process for this plant, he had to go to Belgium for a couple of months to learn their process. So, during his two-month stay, I took a trip over for a couple of weeks. He was staying in an apartment there in Hoogstraten. All day he went to work, and I could either stay at the apartment or I could venture out on foot to sightsee, which I did occasionally, but I was afraid I would get lost, so I wouldn't venture too far.

There were, from my recollection, a few businesses and very small but well-built, modest homes… a very quiet and humble feel. I also remember how surprised I was to find that almost everyone owned a bicycle, and that was their major means of transportation. I thought it was an awesome way to bring up a child and to live as opposed to the hustle and bustle of everyone rushing around in cars back home. It was a small town, and not much to see, but there was an awesome, picturesque church a few blocks from the apartment.

Honestly, that church is the most memorable thing about this town and my trip to me. It seemed so huge compared to its surroundings. So, I ventured inside and was very surprised to find, as was being described to me, that there was a sectioned-off area called a confessional so that you could go in it and discuss any of your sins and confess them. The scary part was that there was someone that you were confessing to on the other side of the confessional. I was asked if I wanted to do this, and I was also told about the scripture, "Confess your sins one to another, and the truth will set you free." Wow... I remember thinking that I was in a country where no one knew me, not even this pastor or rabbi or whatever he was referred to, and I wouldn't be talked about or gossiped about or looked down upon if I confessed! I decided I needed and wanted to confess my sins so I could be set free! So, I can recall sitting in this booth, and all I could see was the face, mainly the eyes, of the person I was confessing to. I had total belief and total trust in the fact I had shared my sins with this person and that the Lord would forgive me! It was my secret, and I was sure I was both forgiven and set free!

Well, while I was on this trip to see and be with my husband, I can also remember being somewhat perplexed and feeling that my husband would have actually preferred that I wasn't there. I can't put my finger on it, even to this day, but he didn't seem at all to be as excited about the fact that I had left our two small children for a couple of weeks to come and spend some alone and quality time with him as I thought he would be.

We did, however, make a couple of trips. We went to Holland and had a tour guide, a coworker of his, who showed us the inner workings of Holland and especially the windmills. I was shocked to find that marijuana was being smoked on the streets and no one was being locked up. I was also shocked to find out that there were houses with windows where you shop for a lady that was in the window to be bought for the evening!

Anyway, we also made our way to Paris for a day. I was utterly amazed at the architecture and the thought of how long ago it was built and the beauty that was ever present no matter which way you looked.

Well, I returned to the states for him to continue his training. Something I never understood was that when he returned, he came up around two thousand short of receipts when he had to do his expense report. He had to share that with me because he had to come up with the difference but couldn't come up with a reason as to why and how he could not justify a two-thousand-dollar shortage in receipts. We were maxed out on the credit cards we had together because his thought process was if he wanted it, we could just put it on a card and pay later. We had many disagreements about that, which began as soon as we were married. That thought process had begun early on in our marriage whenever he wanted marijuana, or other drugs, as it turned out to be, of course, that we could just pay later. So, I had to put the two grand that he could not account for on my credit union card that I had.

There were a lot of changes that had to happen for us to move. We had to find a new home in a new town again, but this time was a little different than the two times before. This time we had two small children to bring along. Our daughter was now six, and our son was three.

Well, we had moved from South Carolina to a small town an hour's drive west of Macon. So, there we were in a new town with no friends, and I still had no one to talk to but the kids. My husband was still an avid tennis player, and it wasn't long before he found the tennis courts and the tennis groups to spend most of his spare time with. I busied myself with our home and our children, again. He, on the other hand, worked and played tennis most of the time, again. We had moved to a big home, rent-to-buy option. It had five acres of land, a barn, a garage, and lots of grass. I busied myself with keeping the grass cut, the weed eating, the bushes hedged, and the trees trimmed. It would take me about thirteen hours just to cut the grass. Good thing I had been taught to do hard work at an early age, or this would not have been doable. When we first moved there, I was afraid to ride a mower, so I pushed it to start with. It didn't take me but a couple of times to realize I needed to ride a mower. I did all the work around the house. The house was spotless every Friday so that I didn't have to work to keep it clean on the weekend so I could spend any time he allowed us with him. Our weekend time usually consisted of movie after movie after movie. Of course, the movies weren't kid-friendly most of the time, so the kids would have to busy themselves at play… together. He would come home with a pile of movies for the weekend, every weekend. That was his favorite pass time unless he was playing tennis or Tetris, which he would play for hours. He came home for lunch every day, and once lunch was eaten, he would play Tetris until time to go back to work. Anytime I would even so much as ask him to fix the kids a drink, you would think the world had come to an end. So, needless to say, we were still picture perfect but far… far from it.

For some reason, my husband began to suggest that we start going to church. Well, his suggestions took me back to 1975 when my employer asked me to be his lover. Remember, I shared what this made me think of church-goers. So I, in my mind, would wonder for what. However, this urging of his did spark a thought process in me. I began to ask the Lord, or question the Lord, "If You are for real, I need You to do something in my life to show me because I don't want to go to church because it is something I am supposed to do, but I want to go to church knowing and believing in You!" Well, this story I am about to share is how the Lord not only answered my prayer but did it in a way that spoke volumes to me! The story you are about to read was published in the small hometown paper as a result of a conversation I had with one of the editors of the paper after my mom passed. I had called to offer my assistance because there was an article on the front page about a man who was dying of cancer and needed help. I began to share this story, and she said it was beautiful. I asked if she wanted to write it. She said, "No, I want you to." Well, here is the story…

Before you read the story, there are a few things I want you to know…

I was the only child out of six that wasn't working at the time, so I was able to spend the last two weeks of my mom's life with her. I had gone yard selling with her the week before I got the call from my Diddy telling me the cancer was back. I explained to him that it couldn't be because she was well... a week ago. He explained to me that she was on the couch, unable to move. He also expressed to me that he was scared and alone. This was the first time in my life when I had actually heard fear in my Diddy's voice. Before we hung up, something utterly unexpected and out of the blue happened! My Diddy... told me that he loved me! I hung up the phone and burst into tears and sobbed! My children, then nine and six, were watching TV in the room where the phone was and overheard the conversation. They couldn't help but notice and questioned me as to why I was crying and asked if Meemaw was dying and if that was why I was crying. The real reason I was crying was actually both, but the overwhelming reason at the time was because I finally heard the words come from my father that I had longed for all my life. And I didn't say it first, which made it even more powerful and meaningful and emotional to me! You see, I had actually told Mom many years before when I was in the accident that totaled my car when I worked for the man at the exterminating company. I had been upset, for some time, about the fact that my family didn't say those words because my husband's family did. Those were words that I had never heard, and they seemed to flow so easily from one another... in his family... and even to me! So, I realized I could have easily been killed that day, as I talked to my mom, and before I hung up, I said those words, and much to my surprise... she said them back!

Well, I didn't want to go back to Mom and Dad's because it was too hard, I thought... on me! She had been hospitalized that night after Dad called me and was diagnosed with dehydration. She had told the doctors to be honest with her and tell her what was going on. I had arrived and was alone with her the next day after she was actually told by the doctors that she had two to six months to live. She shared with me that she was worried about one of my brothers; he happened to be on duty the night she passed. He happened to be there, but not without some help from my brother and me. We had to go and find him because he wasn't coming around and still had to be coaxed to come in.

The following is an article in the Thomaston, Georgia, paper because of me calling a journalist that had shared a story and picture of a man suffering from the ravages of cancer, and she also shared some of his needs. I began sharing about what I had just gone through, and the journalist said, "That is beautiful." I asked if she would like to write a story about it, and she said, "No, I want you to."

Guest Comment: "Wonderful Things Do Happen Even to the Terminally Ill" by Trish Bagwell

My mother was operated on almost one year ago for stomach cancer, weighing approximately 150 pounds before surgery. They removed her stomach, three-fourths of her pancreas, part of her spleen, and some lymph nodes. She then went through six months of chemotherapy. After the chemo, she was about to take her radiation treatments, and she began to have really bad pains in her stomach area (she didn't have a stomach anymore, just a small pouch). All kinds of tests were run after the doctors had just been telling her it was probably just gas. The test results finally showed that the cancer was back, this time consuming her intestines. I received a call from my father with this news, and my husband took me up that night (one hour and a half from Thomaston to a small town called Loganville).

When I walked in the door, my mother (whom I had just seen three weeks before and had gone shopping and cooked with) was lying on the couch, barely capable of moving. The next day we took her to the doctor, and they put her in the hospital for dehydration. On Thursday, when she questioned the doctor for the truth, her doctor told her there was nothing they could do; she had two to three months to live.

On Saturday, she came home. We arranged a hospital bed, wheelchair, and porta pot through hospice. On Monday, my sister (Carol) and I decided to put her in the tub; we thought it would make her feel better. We walked her wobbly, frail eighty-nine-pound body to the bathroom and put her in the tub. This was a bad choice, as after about two minutes, she told me she had to get out; it hurt so bad. She began to be sick, and two small tears rolled from each corner of her eyes down her cheeks. I got a tissue and wiped them away for her. My father had to help her out of the tub while I got the wheelchair (after composing myself—as I went into another room and cried for a moment, because that was all I had.)

I had to come home after this episode to be here to pick my children up from school on Monday. My husband came home for lunch shortly after I got there, and I cried and shared this story with him. He told me to pack my bags and not worry about him and the kids and go take care of my mother. I told him I didn't want to go, that it was too hard for me to see her this way. Nevertheless, he convinced me to go and help and not think about myself and my pain but my mother's and father's, because they were alone during the day and night.

So, the next day I went back. My father and I were lifting, picking up, and taking care of her the best we knew how. On my first night back, my father slept on the couch and I on another, in the room with her. The second night my sister (Carol) and I stayed with her. That night she seemed to be trying to raise her hands. Carol asked her what she was doing. My mother said, "I want to raise my hands," Carol said, "Do you want me to help you?" My mother said, "Yes." So, Carol took one hand and I the other and raised them up for her, elbows still on the bed. Carol said, "What are you doing?" Mother said, "Reaching." Carol said, "Reaching for what?" Mother replied, "Reaching for the sky!" When she said this, we raised her arms to the sky as high as we could reach. We began to cry and tell her how much we loved and were going to miss her—and she did the same. We let her know we would help her reach because we loved her and we didn't want her to suffer.

The next day, which was Wednesday, my brother Randy, my dad, and I were there. She came to and told my dad, "I'm going to die, Pawpaw." My dad had begun to encourage her and told her she wasn't going to die; she was getting better. She said again, "I'm going to die." She then got sick again, and we worked to help her as best we could. When she got okay, my dad walked to the kitchen and poured him a cup of coffee. I walked in and put my arm over his shoulder, and asked if he was alright. He said "yes" with tear-filled eyes. I expressed to him that he could not tell her she wasn't going to die. "She knows she is, and she knows you know she is." The hospice people and everyone had expressed how important it is to give them permission to die. I told him, "You have to give her permission and let her know it's okay." He said, "I know, but it's hard." I told him I knew how hard it was, and I told him of my sister's and my experience the night before. I was summoned back to the room by my brother, telling me that Mother was saying she wanted to hear her "first gospel song." After being questioned by all of us as to the name of it, all we could get her to say was, "My first gospel song." Finally, my dad said, "Mom, we don't know what it is; do you want us to sing you a song?" She replied, "Yes." So, we all three looked at one another, with a question of what to sing. I said, "How about 'Amazing Grace'?" She said, "Okay."

So, the three of us cried-sang "Amazing Grace" to her, and my father gave her his permission and acceptance of the future at this time. During this episode, there was a friend (of my parents) who had come to visit. She had brought her sister (who is a homecare nurse). After singing to our mother, the three of us were kind of in a daze. The visitor, who was the homecare nurse, jumped right up at this time and began to administer care to my mother. She fed her (more than we had been able to get her to eat in days). She began to ask me for things, and I got them. She asked for a flat sheet to put up under my mother, which she explained would be a swing for her body so we could lift her, roll her over, make up her bed, and not hurt Mother nor my father or me anymore. My dad and I watched and saw the response this "wonderful woman" (that's what I call her, and I also felt she was an angel sent from the Lord) was getting from my mother. (Later, she went to her car to smoke, and even though I didn't like smoke, I went and got in the car with her and asked for her to educate me!) She told me a list of things I needed to get to take good care of my mother. My dad and I never questioned for one moment whether we should listen to her or not. I went right away and got everything on the list. She fed me so much information in a matter of an hour and a half and showed me what to do for my mom for her problems, and I became a vacuum, and then I became a teacher for my siblings and their husbands and wives, as everybody pitched in, in some way or another.

From that time on, someone was with her around the clock. Many times during this period, she would ask, "Somebody tell me what's going on." We would simply say she was sick and we were taking care of her. She was able to tell us of her needs until about two days prior to her death. There were occasions when she asked, "What was all of them pretty dresses hanging around?" "Who was that strange man?" "Why so far away?"

On Saturday, prior to her death on Sunday night, she refused (to my dad, my sister, and me) her medication, which was morphine at this time; from 5:10 a.m. to around 2:00 p.m., she did not have any. At about 11 a.m. on Saturday, I was checking on her fever, pain, and asking if she wanted medicine. She asked me, "Tell me what's going on." So, I did.

I told her she was dying; we didn't want her to, but we did not want her to hurt and suffer anymore. I told her that she had been to the place she needed to go because she had questioned us about the pretty dresses, and the strange man, and why so far away. I told her we had not had any pretty dresses, nor was there a strange man, so the next time she went there, we wanted her to stay. Through all this, she was answering me with okays and goods. I told her we wanted her to die a peaceful death by just losing her breath, but not a horrible death by drowning in her vomit. She all the while saying "okay" and "good," now seeming at ease with death.

I then called my dad into the room and told him of her alertness and answering everything you would say. He talked to her and looked at me in amazement. I then got my sister, then my youngest brother, Johnny. Then my brother Randy and his family pulled up, and he talked with her. Then my brother Roy; he talked. After studying the situation, I realized my brother Ronald (the one she had expressed concern to me about the day after she was told she had two to three months to live) wasn't there. I called him, and he came right over (but still had to be coaxed to come in). So at that time, all six children had a chance to talk to her. After this, each of her grandchildren that were there (thirteen out of fourteen) got to talk to her. Some read Bible verses, and she thanked and hugged some. Others just expressed their love. Also, at midnight on Saturday night, I was checking on her, and I asked if she wanted some crushed ice for her throat. She replied, "The next person that asks me if I want some ice, I'm going to slap the s*** out of 'em!" We all got a good laugh out of that. That night my brother Ronald (the one she was worried about), his wife Pam, and myself (I wasn't supposed to be, but I couldn't sleep) were on duty. At about 4:30 a.m., I went into the kitchen and got the hospice book and turned directly to page twenty-four, which read "The Approaching Signs of Death." I explained to Ronald that I didn't know when it was going to happen, but since he was there, it was best to be prepared and understand what was going on if it did. So, he and I sat with a flashlight and read this along with a sheet of instructions that I had written up of things to do after she passed. We then gave these to his wife, Pam, to read. Not fifteen minutes after we had finished reading, my mother went from a really loud breathing (which she had done all night) to sudden silence. We all jumped up. I began to check her pulse and told Pam to wake my sister up, who was on the couch. She checked her pulse on the other side, and we sent Pam to get dad. He got there just in time to see her last two peaceful breaths and tell her how much he loved her.

Prior to all the godsent people and blessings and miracles, I witnessed during my mother's death I was not a firm believer in the Lord. The following Thursday morning at *about 5:00 a.m., I called the pastor and talked to him until about 7:00 a.m. because I couldn't take it anymore! So, on Sunday, September 27, 1992, I accepted Christ in that pastor's church and was saved along with my husband in a church I had never visited before until one week to the day after the death of my mother by one of the preachers who spoke at my wonderful mothers funeral.*

I would like to dedicate this article to my mother and father; to Ronald, for not passing out and doing an excellent job; to my husband, for sending me back; to my children, for doing without me for two weeks; to all my friends, who helped with my children and clothes; to all the non-believers—may they see the light; and last but not least, to the "wonderful woman" who taught me.

Trish Bagwell's mother died on September 20, 1992. She wanted to share her story with others who may be facing the prospect of losing someone they love to the ravages of cancer and other diseases.

Finding My Horizon

As I said earlier, I was there for two weeks to help my dad, feed, bathe, medicate, and help assist with the normal daily functions. My brothers and sister and in-laws would come and help when they could. We began to work out a schedule for someone to be in the room with her during the nights as well. We had moved her into the den. There were two couches in the room, one on each side of her. I was running on adrenaline, I guess, because I was hardly in need of rest.

My dad and I had been working for days to move her and lift her and actually carry her so she could use the porta pot.

We were both worn out because if you have ever had to experience this, you know that someone who is going through this is unable to lift themselves at all and are basically dead weight, which feels so much heavier.

The night my sister and I were on duty with her, and she began flailing her arms and making so much noise that she woke us up was a very moving and inspiring time, and I felt the Lord was definitely the author of this event and was answering my prayer!

The next day a lady that was just brought to the house by a friend of Mom and Dad's became an angel to me. My oldest brother had come over. Mother had come out of her comatose state and began to ask for her favorite gospel song. Well, none of us, my dad, brother, or me, knew what song she was talking about. We, not being involved in church (and to my knowledge, she had never been involved), didn't have any idea what to sing. We couldn't get anything out of her but that she wanted to hear her favorite. We looked at each other puzzled, and I asked, "How about 'Amazing Grace'?" Honestly, it was the only gospel song that I halfway knew. She said, "Okay." Well, after my dad, brother, and I sang, she got sick! She also began to express that she was going to die. My dad insisted to her that she wasn't. My dad departed the room and went to the kitchen and poured himself a cup of coffee. I left my brother with Mom and went to the kitchen to have a talk with my dad. I asked if he was okay. He said he was, but I could see he wasn't, as he wiped a tear away. I told him that he could not tell her that she was not going to die. I told him what had happened with my sister and me the night before and how we had given her permission. I told him she needed his permission because she felt guilty leaving. He teared up again and told me that he knew, but… it was too hard.

Well, while I was having the conversation with my dad, I could hear the stranger that was in the house taking care of my mom. I heard her being somewhat loud, yet not forceful, but demanding. I saw my mom responding to this stranger, unlike she had been responding to my dad and me. She was listening and doing what the stranger was telling her to do. I said to myself, *This lady knows something that I don't but need to.*

She went to her car to smoke, and even though I didn't smoke and didn't like the smell, I sat in the car with her and quizzed her. I found that she was a home care nurse and did this for a living. She educated me on many things. She told me to call the doctor and get liquid morphine as she had witnessed us beating it with a hammer to make powder so she could swallow it. She taught me about the sheet that you use to lift her and move her around instead of pulling on her like we were. She explained we could break her brittle bones the way we were doing it. She educated me about some cream we needed to prevent bed sores. She educated me, and I educated Dad and the rest. I took a trip to the drug store and called the doctor and got and did everything she had taught me. She was our saving grace… our angel in disguise! More of the Lord answering my prayer!

Education was the key to our success! Our goal was to give her a peaceful death, and with this angel's help, we were able to do that!

The day Mom passed, I had been trying to give her medication to her the night before, and she told me she didn't want it. I was apprehensive, but nevertheless, I did what she asked. I had tried to wake her a couple of times, and the last time I did, I asked if she wanted her meds or something to drink; she kindly but adamantly told me, "The next person that asks me if I want it, I am going to slap 'the s***' out of them." That was sign enough for me. You see, I had been slapped in the face one time in my life by my mom, and I can remember, to this day, how hurtful it was.

So, my mom was not given her assigned dose of morphine as prescribed by the doctor but as unsubscribed by her. I shared this with no one at the time.

The next day, Mom was about herself and knew everything that was going on and was able to have conversations with us. I witnessed every one of my siblings pull up one by one without being called and told she was cohesive. That was another miracle to me! I can remember just sitting back and watching… in amazement! Eventually, all siblings and thirteen out of fourteen of the grandchildren all ironically showed up. Even my brother, the one she was worried about. He was there, outside, but wasn't coming in even though my brother and I had gone and found him days before and explained to him he needed to come. So, we went out to talk to him some more. He shared he just wanted to remember her the way she was, not sick. I asked if he had ever told her that he loved her… or vice versa. He said no. I told him he might never be able to if he didn't do it then because no one knew how long she would be there. He told me we were torturing her. I explained to him what our goal was. I explained she asked me for some oatmeal that morning, and I fixed it, but she was only able to take a few bites. What mattered to me was that she asked, and I gave. He finally came in, and when he did, he immediately just knelt by her bed and told her he loved her, and she did the same. I was witnessing from the kitchen as I wanted him to have that time alone with her. As he was visiting, she got sick. I had already told him that we were suctioning her when she got sick so she wouldn't choke. He graciously and lovingly… did his job!

As I stood in the kitchen and witnessed this, it was another of the most beautiful and touching moments in my mom's passing. The love shared between mom and son and the thought of knowing that she was worried about him… instead of herself! And they were now sharing their love with one another.

Well, when the sickness passed, we all stood around her bedside and sang to her. I remember we sang "Jesus Loves Me." I don't remember if we sang something else. "Jesus Loves Me" was a song I was feeling deep within my heart and soul as I sang it… with a renewed and vibrant sense of the true meaning of the song!

After all this excitement, my mom began to express how much pain she was in and that it even hurt when someone touched the bed.

I told my sister that she hadn't had her medication because she didn't want it. She got mad at me, but I was okay with that because my mom had not been lying there comatose while everyone visited. She had a wonderful visit with everyone, and everyone had a wonderful visit with her. She and the son she was so worried about had a moment that needed to happen. Little did we know, it was ours and hers last meaningful visit! Upon receiving her medication, she became comatose the rest of the day and into the evening.

That night was the night that the son she was worried about said he would be on duty along with his wife. My sister was in the room with them too, and I was to sleep in the living room. I lay there, unable to sleep, and got up and went and visited with my brother and his wife.

Although my sister was in the room, she was fast asleep. I explained to them that no one knew when it would happen, but since they were on duty that night, I wanted to prepare them in case it did happen. I took a flashlight and had them read the hospice book we had been given on page twenty-four. "The Approaching Signs of Death" was the name of this chapter. This chapter or section explained not only the approaching signs but what would take place afterward. They both read this with the flashlight as we didn't want to turn on the lights. I think within fifteen minutes or less, after they read it and we sat whispering and talking in the dark… my mom went from the heavy breathing she had been doing all night to utter silence.

My sister, my brother, his wife, and I were there and at the last moment and in time for her last breath, my father made it to be there with her to witness the life that once was… be there no more!

My brother, who my mom was worried about, was not only there but was also prepared to see the end of her life. I, on the other hand, was blessed to see both. Both my brother be prepared, and my mom be at peace for the fact that the child she was worried about most was there to see her through the end of her life.

Sometimes I feel that my mom gave up her life to save mine, but then I think, *She would have done that; that is what a mother would do!* But I wouldn't give anything for the time I spent with her and the time the Lord spent with us! He used this tragedy to answer my prayer to Him! It was through the many miraculous and beautiful things that happened during my mother's last two weeks and up until her last breath that brought me to a heightened awareness of something greater and more powerful than just us in this world! Amen!

Wonderful Things Do Happen Even to the Terminally Ill!

My Mom was diagnosed with a deadly disease,
And our only agenda was to ensure she passed with ease,
Two to six months was the very short time that she was given,
But only two weeks passed, and then she was no longer living!
If you were given that information as a diagnosis,
Would you spend that time wisely and enjoy the prognosis?
We were all truly blessed beyond compare,
When not only I but the entire family showed up there,
On the day that none of us knew would be her last,
And that her existence would become part of the past!
Although she is gone and lives no more,
I believe she was used by the Lord to open the door,
The door that had been closed so many years before,
Because it was Satan's plan to destroy this testimony,
So, I could not be blessed because I thought church and the
  Lord were phony!
Church is only the earthly Lord's thrown,
But it is up to each of us the seeds that get sewn,
The example we set is all that may be seen,
By those who enter and look to us for what it all means!
If we are the salt of the earth that we are commissioned to be,

Then oh what wonders we will all witness and see!
As I said before, I feel that my mom would have given her life,
So that the Lord could use this time to heal me from strife,
And that is exactly what happened on that beautiful day,
That I believed in the Lord and knew that I could be saved,
And I also knew, beyond a shadow of a doubt, that He had
    answered my prayer!
I also knew, beyond a shadow of doubt, that He listened to me,
    and He also cared!
So, from Sunday to Thursday, I was a bundle of nerves,
Because I knew that I both wanted and that I deserved,
The salvation that only He could offer to me,
Was something I had been searching for and could now see!
So, at the 5 a.m. hour on Thursday morn,
I called a pastor and talked for hours until I knew I was
    reborn!
So, on Sunday I went up and confessed that I believed,
And from that day forward, it has been hard to conceive,
The many changes in my life that have occurred,
Are being shared in this book so they wouldn't become blurred,
Because the gifts that I have now been given,
Cause me to feel that it is the first time in my life… I have
    truly been living!!
Amen!

Written on September 23, 2015, at 9:15 p.m.
Written especially for my mom, Christine,
who was buried September 20, 1992!

My Life was saved, along with many other blessings, as a result of
Mom's passing, hence the title of this poem.

CHAPTER 6
Hidden Secrets Revealed

1993–1997: Ages Thirty-Seven Through Forty-One

Well, as I shared earlier, seven days after the funeral of my mom, I was at the church of the pastor who spoke at her funeral and whom I had called at 5 a.m. in the morning, and I went up to accept Christ as my savior. As I motioned for my husband to move to allow me out, he moved, but then he followed me. So here we were, the two of us, up in front of all these people, who also included my entire family, and we accepted Christ together! I was surprised that he had followed me as he had shared nothing about his desire to do so with me, but nonetheless, I was excited!

Well, we had to go home that evening as I had stayed for another entire week to make sure all things were handled with my dad. He had asked me to remove Mom's things from their bedroom. He gave me a few specific things he wanted to keep, but the rest was removed.

While driving home with our son in the car with me, and our daughter in the car with my husband, I almost had a terrible wreck. I pulled out in front of a car at a four-lane intersection. I was distracted singing, trying to stay awake because the sleep deprivation was hitting me, and I was thinking and telling our son that we would beat my husband as he had taken a different route. I saw this car swerve over to the other side of the road right in front of me and thought, *What in the world are they doing?* It took me a second to realize they were trying not to hit me in the side, going more than fifty miles an hour as I was supposed to have waited on them. They ended up in the other two lanes, turned all the way around. When the police arrived, I shared where my mind was and apologized and told them what I had just been through. The people in the car were so nice and understanding and insisted that no ticket was necessary.

We returned to our small town, where life was going to be different. I was so excited and felt a sense of new awakening. The article you read earlier was published. We had found a church in our town by way of a friend I had made at Mother's Morning Out, where I was taking the kids to the library for reading and craft time. She had invited me before all this had happened, so it seemed only appropriate that we go the following Sunday. This was a big church with about one thousand members at the time. It seemed to be a good fit, so we began being there every time the doors were open. I was pleased when one of the ladies even invited us to Sunday school. I felt a sense of belonging... actually being invited into something.

So here is where this part of the story should be awesome. But unfortunately, my sense of happiness was very short-lived. You see, I began to get lots of compliments and acknowledgment about the article that you read about my mom. My husband was always very quiet and distant if he was present when this happened. One day I received a phone call from a man who described himself as a seventy-year-old man who lived alone after his wife had passed, but when he read my article, he said, "I shouted hallelujah and praise the Lord." He further described his concern for the world and the younger generation. We had a wonderful conversation while my husband listened from across the room. As soon as I hung up, my husband abruptly advised me that I was "wigging out." I asked him what he was talking about, and he advised me that I was "living a fallacy." I was very dismayed at his reaction, but I remember thinking to myself, *He didn't get what I got.* I wasn't wigging out, and I wasn't living a fallacy... I was simply living and believing in Christ! I just let what he said go, as I knew I couldn't change anything, but on the other hand... I knew what I knew and was sad that it didn't seem that he did. But I also rejoiced in the fact that now I felt that I had two fathers that loved me.

My earthly father had told me for the first time in my life that he loved me!

And my heavenly Father had answered my prayers to show me that He loves me!

I was on cloud nine!

And nothing was going to change that!

So, here we are again, picture-perfect! We delved into the church together. He became the RA leader for the young boys, and I became the nursery leader. He was very poignant in Sunday school and loved sharing all his biblical knowledge and percentages with the class as he began to study a lot. I, on the other hand, was the quiet and reserved wife.

There were two people that really stood out to me in that church. One was the music minister. He had an awesome presence about him, and as I described to him, you could see Jesus in his presence, and I wanted that also.

There was a beautiful lady, who was probably in her mid-fifties, I guessed, who seemed to have something that I wanted also. I remember seeing her walking across a plain white wall, and I remember thinking, *I don't know who she is or what it is she has, but I want it.* Later, I understood what she had that I wanted, and it was confidence in Christ… she knew who she was in Christ.

Well, to this day, the music minister still exudes Christ's presence… and thankfully, I have been told I do also. And to this day, the beautiful red-headed lady is my friend, confidant, mentor, and editor, and she and others have encouraged me to write this book and explained that my confidence in Christ is present!

Anyway, for many years we pressed on. He worked, played tennis, and went to church. I stayed home with the children, went to Mother's Morning Out at the library, and went to church. I made some wonderful friends at the library but made no real connections with the women at church other than my library friend and my mentor, who was fifteen years my senior, but we seemed to be of the same age, especially in spirit. We would talk for hours on the phone and just enjoy each other's stories and spirits.

Since I was a stay-at-home mom and needed some friends, and so did my kids, I felt within the church, I asked my mentor if she would start a Bible study so I could build some relationships. There were several stay-at-home moms with kids in the church. We agreed that she would lead, and I would fill in if ever she wasn't able. We started, and she was always there and able to fulfill that position, and I was thankful. I didn't think I would be comfortable doing it anyway with women who were my peers and had been in church way longer than myself, who knew way more than I did.

Well, one morning, she called and said she was unable to attend and needed me to lead. I had already been feeling and had shared with her that although I enjoyed the Bible study, I didn't feel I was making any connections with the ladies. Well, this morning, I had been planning on sharing a concern I had with them. I was concerned about my daughter because there were no other girls in her age group in her Sunday school class, and I felt she needed some other girls and was trying to figure out what to do… maybe even changing churches. I wanted them to show concern and talk me out of it.

The ladies all came in together, around eight to ten of them, and they were all giggling and laughing and discussing some party they had all been to… together. It immediately came over me that they not only were sharing the fun they had, but they had intentionally had it without me. I couldn't hold back the tears. But, at the same time, I said to myself that I would tell them I was crying about the situation with my daughter, which I did. I didn't want them to know that they had hurt me because I felt they wouldn't care... that is why they did it in the first place. They, of course, seemed a little concerned for me and my daughter's situation. But they also said to one another to share what they were all laughing about. So, they continued to share that one of the ladies in the group had just bought a new home and wanted to decorate it in modern style. So they chose the quietest, most conservative girl to bring her the most country, hideous present at her house warming party in order to see her reaction and then share their secret with her and have the laugh that they were continuing to have at her reaction.

It was hard for me to lead this Bible study, but with the Lord's assistance, I managed. As I left and was driving away alone with my thoughts, but not alone because my children were with me, I asked the Lord why. I asked the Lord why they would do this to me and why they would choose to share it with me like that, as it was obvious that I was the only one in the room that wasn't invited. The Lord answered me by saying, "I have something better than this for you." That was all I needed to hear. I never worried again. I couldn't care less if they wanted to be my friend or not. I no longer wanted or needed to be theirs!

As time passed, one of the Bible study ladies turned to me at fellowship time one day. We had sat side by side with our families for a long time, and she would always stand and turn her back to me and never turn around, but on this day, she did, and she said to me, "I know why everyone thinks you are so pretty; it's your personality." I can remember thinking, *You just told me volumes.* She was very attractive, but I felt she just told me what the entire ordeal was all about...

Jealousy!

What's funny is I never knew everyone thought I was so pretty, as she described. And I couldn't care less that they thought I was. Beauty is more than skin or surface deep.

My daughter sent me a text one day, by Audrey Hepburn, that says it perfectly…

Makeup can make you beautiful on the outside, but it does nothing for the inside, unless you eat the makeup!

You see, both she and her sister were very attractive, and they were the "center of the ladies," and if you weren't their friend, you weren't anybody. I wasn't the only one that wasn't allowed in their group. Fortunately, though, I didn't allow them to run me off because of their behavior, as they did some, and to this day, they probably don't even know it. But I wonder… would they even really care?

The ladies' Bible study was dissolved not long after this as it was hard for not only me to continue but my mentor as well, as some of her daughters were affected as well. We did try to continue and teach, but to no avail. So, I went back to being a stay-at-home mom with my kids, my library friends, my mentor, and my busy husband.

My husband had still been active at church with the RA's, actively speaking up all the time in Sunday school and helping organize the men of the church to participate in the Promise Keepers. I had asked my husband if he would teach me how to use the computer. Since I didn't work, I didn't know anything about a computer, so he showed me how to use Microsoft Word.

I had been thinking about an Easter play that would be so cute for the young kids. I would think about it and say to myself that someone needed to do it. I would think, and I would dismiss it as someone else's duty. The thoughts persisted, and I dismissed my thoughts by saying I was too busy, and besides that, I didn't know enough about the Bible to write the story. The thoughts persisted. So, one day I was sitting on the front porch swing, and the thoughts were back. I just said a prayer; I said, "Lord, if this is from You, then do something, so I will know, and I will do it because I don't want to do it if it is of me, but I will do it if it is from You." I said that prayer and left and went to the store at the top of the road, and my bill totaled $7.77. I said, "Okay."

Below is the result of my $7.77 confirmation!

I woke up around 1 a.m. one morning, and in just a little while, this was written!

It was performed for about three years on Easter morning at my church!

Even if it is their first time to be there, kids are on stage doing a play about Easter!

How beautiful is that... like I said, it wasn't from me!

First, I'll share the letter I sent to the pastor telling him about the events that transpired.

March 22, 1995

Pastor Rex,

The Lord laid this on my heart to do for Easter back in August of last year, one day while I was sitting on the front porch swinging with Kaitlyn. I questioned Him at that time as to whether it was from Him or from me, because I told Him that if it was from me, I didn't want to do it. I said, "Lord, let me know if it's from You." Shortly thereafter, I had to go to the grocery store (which was a convenience store at the top of the road), and my bill totaled $7.77! I immediately said, "Thank You, Lord, I know that's my sign—not coincidence."

Time passed, and I went to work, and Easter was rapidly approaching. I tried to tell myself that I was too busy for this. Work, Kaitlyn, soccer, girl scouts, and anything else I could use to make myself feel better about not doing it.

The Lord really laid it on my heart again during revival. Now here it is, about three weeks away from Easter, and I finally quit being so stubborn and sat down at the computer around 1:00 a.m., He woke me up with it on my mind, and I-He-we finished it in a very short while, thanks to the Lord, because I told Him that He was going to have to do it for me—and He did. It would have taken me forever!

Enclosed is a copy of the play for your approval. Let me know if it's okay to do, so I can get started with the children right away. Although it will be really easy for them because all they will have to do is some hand motions and gestures. If there is anything you don't like, take it out, or anything you want to change, change it. If you approve, pray that it will touch some lost soul in the congregation—there will probably be many on Easter. I know, as a lost sinner myself—that was one day out of the year I found myself in church.

Trish

P.S. Thanks for the incentive—to give God,
what He gives you.

The Love Story
(An Easter Play)

NARRATOR: We would like to present to you our rendition of the Bible, which we call "The Love Story."

NARRATOR: In the beginning, God created light
CHILDREN: (Eyes closed, open widely)

NARRATOR: The sky above.
CHILDREN: (Raise hands, to one side, toward the sky)

NARRATOR: Land, / and seas, / plants and trees.

(/ = pause between each for children's motions)

CHILDREN: (Wave hand palm down as land; wavy motion with hands as seas; hands in the air, making wavy motions as plants and trees)

NARRATOR: Sun, / moon, and stars. (/ = pause described above)

CHILDREN: (Squint; un-squint look to the sky)

NARRATOR: All creations, great and small!

CHILDREN: (Arms stretched wide = great; bring together hands almost touching = small)

NARRATOR: The cattle on a thousand hills.

CHILDREN: (Say "moo")

NARRATOR: Mankind—the image of God, Adam/ (pause) and Eve.

CHILDREN: (Boys stand, pause, boys sit; girls stand, pause, girls sit.)

NARRATOR: On the seventh day, God rests.

CHILDREN: (Fold arms, yawn)

NARRATOR: In the Garden of Eden, God judges the first sin.

CHILDREN: (Represent the thinker)

NARRATOR: God exiles Adam and Eve from the garden.

CHILDREN: (Wave hand with a sweeping away motion; sad face)

NARRATOR: Mankind turns to murder, Cain, and Abel.

CHILDREN: (Make tsk-tsk sound)

NARRATOR: God was very displeased with mankind.
CHILDREN: (Shake head no)

NARRATOR: He could only find one righteous man, Noah.
CHILDREN: (Hold one finger up)

NARRATOR: God prepared Noah for the Great Flood—
Noah builds an Ark as a haven for his family
CHILDREN: (Girls make hammer motions—boys make saw motions)

NARRATOR: Noah took his family and two of each animal on the ark.
CHILDREN: (Hold two fingers up)

NARRATOR: It rained for forty days and forty nights and covered the whole earth with water.
CHILDREN: (Represent raining with fingers)

NARRATOR: All was washed away but Noah's ark, and after many days the rain dried up.
CHILDREN: (Represent rain rising—palms up, raise arms)

NARRATOR: The world was good again, until many years passed.
CHILDREN: (Shake head yes and smile big)

NARRATOR: God sends an angel from heaven to tell of our Savior.
CHILDREN: (Raise hands toward heaven to one side)

NARRATOR: Jesus, our Savior, is born!
CHILDREN: (Cradle baby motion)

NARRATOR: Jesus grows from a baby to a man.
CHILDREN: (Cradle baby, raise one hand high)

NARRATOR: Jesus performs many miracles for us—the blind can see!

CHILDREN: (Close eyes, open wide)

NARRATOR: The lame can walk!

CHILDREN: (Walk in place, surprised)

NARRATOR: The afflicted are cured!

CHILDREN: (Look all over your body, surprised)

NARRATOR: The dead live again!

CHILDREN: (Say "Lazarus come forth")

NARRATOR: Time goes by, and the world turns on Jesus.

CHILDREN: (Shake head no; make tsk-tsk sound)

NARRATOR: God allows this to happen so that we may believe in Jesus and be forgiven of our sins.

CHILDREN: (Shake head yes, vigorously)

NARRATOR: Jesus is crucified!

CHILDREN: (Point to cross)

NARRATOR: Three days pass, and Jesus lives again!

CHILDREN: (Hold three fingers up, be happy)

NARRATOR: The occasion that we celebrate today!

CHILDREN: (Point to cross, show church, show your clothes)

NARRATOR: Easter! The resurrection of Jesus!

CHILDREN: (Point to cross, palms up, make rising motion)

NARRATOR: Just as He came back again then, we are promised His return again one day!

CHILDREN: (Shake head yes, vigorously)

NARRATOR: For it is written that one day the eastern sky will part!

CHILDREN: (Look to sky, hands raised overhead together, burst them apart)

NARRATOR: The trumpet of the archangel will blow!

CHILDREN: (Represent blowing a trumpet)

NARRATOR: And all who are saved will join Jesus in Heaven—our eternal home forever and forever and forever!

CHILDREN: (Exit using arms as wings, flying away motion)

SINGER: Sings "I'll Fly Away" (sang the first year of play being performed) *OR*

SINGER AND CHILDREN: Sing this song I wrote the next year sang to the "Care Bear" tune:

"WHO'S THAT"

Who's that coming from somewhere up in the sky?
It's Jesus Christ, and He's coming for you and I!
It's the day of the rapture; now, we'll be with Him forever after!
No more pain and sorrow, no, not even fear, He'll wipe away every tear!
We will have joy in our hearts, and from us, He will never part!

(Say)... ... ...
We will sit around His feet; PLEASE don't you miss this treat!
Who's that coming from somewhere up in the sky?
Who's that coming from somewhere up in the sky?

Who's that coming from somewhere up in the sky?

(Say)... ... ...(Point)

IT'S JESUS CHRIST, and He's coming for YOU AND I!!!

This play was performed for several years!
Praise the Lord for the inspiration! Amen

What you just read turned out to be the first play I wrote for the church. I couldn't understand when my mentor told me one day that the Valentine's banquet was just around the corner. She finished by saying, "I know I want something with telephones... see what you can come up with." I remember hanging up the phone and saying out loud to myself, "What in the world does she want from me? I don't know anything." Well, she got her skit, and it was with phones. It was a phone conversation between two women, and one did all the talking while the other tried to get a word in edgewise... and she was always trying. It was also another early morning skit that was written in a very short while. I had a very small part but was so scared to do it, but I managed because it was just the introduction. Although, I was very nervous, like I had been the only other time I had to speak in front of people. I had to speak in front of girl scouts and their parents a few years before, and I was so nervous my knees were shaking. I didn't like being the center of attention... at all!

And, of course, the next Valentine's came around, and my mentor asked me again for a skit. I did and said the same thing to myself as I got off the phone with her, "What does she want from me, and why does she do this? I don't know anything!" Well, I walked by my bookcase after hanging up, and a book jumped out at me. Not literally, of course, but figuratively speaking. It was a book that I had never touched again once it went on the shelf because of the way it was presented to me. You see, one day, my husband came in and shoved it in my face and callously explained that he had bought me a present. He said, "It is about the blessing, and you didn't get it as a child, and you need to read it." He further explained that it was about parents giving the blessing, and I needed to read it because I didn't get the blessing. Well, that was no way to present a present! A present is supposed to make you feel good. But instead, the presentation only made me think, *And you think you did get the blessing!* I also thought, *It will be a cold day in, well, you know where, before I read that book!* Well, that day, it was a cold day there... I guess!

I picked that book up and took it with me to the study (restroom). The book was called *The Blessing* by Gary Smalley and John Trent, PhD. Well, I went straight to the contents to read the chapter headings. Chapter twelve captured me right away for the possibility of a play. It was entitled "A Church that Gives the Blessing." I read chapter twelve and was blessed so much that I read the entire book. Chapter twelve, however, became the basis for the Valentine's skit for this year. The skit was written, which also included the Beatitudes, and it was also written the same as before. I was awakened early in the morning, and it was written in a very short while. I was so excited and tried to share with my husband what the Lord was doing and showing me. My husband, however, reiterated to me the same statement, and more, that he had with me when the elderly gentlemen and I hung up from our wonderful Christ-praising conversation about the article I wrote. My husband boldly and adamantly explained to me that I was wigging out and that the Lord was not showing me anything and explained to me that the Lord didn't use women. Ironically, I had been studying the Bible the night before he said that to me, that the Lord didn't use women, and I had studied all about Deborah. So, after he said that, I asked him, "What about Deborah?" He said, "Who is Deborah?" I said, "The Lord chose her to lead Israel." He said he had never heard of her. I was pleased because he was always making it a point to let me and everyone else around know how much he knew. Yet, this time, I knew something that he didn't. This time when he was adamantly telling me that the Lord had not, would not, and most certainly wasn't showing me anything, but I knew better!

I believed then and still do, beyond a shadow of a doubt, that the Lord had led me to the scripture about Deborah, especially since it was the night before I needed to know it!

The year before, when I did the Valentine's skit, it really caused a strain on our marriage. My husband was at the previous skit, but I can remember looking at him and hoping to see approval, but if anything, the look was one of disdain. He wasn't happy that I was doing this at all! But the previous year, I had not shared much about what was going on and how it all came about, but he knew I had written a skit. So, this year he was very disgruntled, and he grudgingly informed me that he would not be at the Valentine's banquet, even though he was signed up and had a spot next to me, and his steak dinner was paid for. So, I had a decision to make. Do I surrender to my husband and his belief that the Lord doesn't use women and surrender to his belief that he ever so prevalently pointed out to me in the Bible, which he had highlighted, by the way, that a woman was supposed to be submissive to her husband? He pointed this out to me many times as he pointed with his finger, over and over and over again, this highlighted statement each time that he wanted to teach me this very important message that he wanted me to understand and abide by. I don't want you to get the wrong idea, but as Christians, if I had a different opinion, or even tried to share an opinion different than he did, this was his way of discussing it with me.

I was surprised to find that he so adamantly opposed to me being used by the Lord, but he had professed many things the Lord had done and showed him, yet since I was a woman, that was impossible! Although, he said he loved to listen to Joyce Meyer, which was confusing. So, you can imagine how torn I was. I felt I was being led and given the gift to write the skits I had written, but my husband was profoundly telling me I was not being led, not being used, and no way should I do what I was doing because the Lord didn't use women. Because I was so torn, I had to lean on the Lord for guidance as to whether this was His will or mine. So, I was in the shower one day, cleansing my body and seeking a spiritual cleansing for my mind, and I prayed to the Lord, "Let me know that You are with me, that You want me to do this, that You will be right beside me or I will be so afraid I won't be able to do it because I will be as nervous as I was when I spoke to the girl scouts and the words will come out so distorted people may think I am speaking in tongues." What happened next was very emotional and so awe-inspiring that I knew beyond a shadow of a doubt that the Lord was answering my prayer! A previous scenario that had happened in my life came vividly to my mind and memory. I felt He spoke to me and said, "Remember when I showed you." I was in a vehicle, on the passenger side, late at night, and in the lights up ahead in the road was a huge possum. The possum was moving ever so slowly across the road. I could see its huge eye and wondered why it acted like it didn't see the headlights approaching. To myself, I began to tell the possum to run, "Don't you see us? You're about to die!" The possum just continued his slow and steady path. I honestly don't remember if it got hit or not. But with that scenario, I was assured that the people would be the headlights and I would be the possum, and I would never see them… the headlights! I was truly amazed, but with this divine revelation from God, as I was later explained, it was from my pastor, I'm sure you can imagine the choice I made.

Yes… I decided to put my faith and trust in the Lord!
I was a possum!
The headlights didn't faze me, either!
My husband, however, was not present as he had advised!

Another thing that strongly helped me make the decision was the fact that while I was using the computer to write the skit… I stumbled on something that caused me great alarm but also caused me to know there was a deeper reason for his behavior and something that I would have to figure out how to get to the bottom of. I found a folder that was entitled "His Confession to Me." I was stunned, but I was also so excited because I thought I had found out something that would answer a lot of questions I had for many years. I always knew there was something I didn't know that caused him to be the way he was. I thought I was finally going to get to know so we could become what Christ would have us be. Well, the folder was locked, and no matter how hard I tried, I couldn't get in it to see the contents that I so desperately needed to see! I must wait until the right time and go about it in the right way to find out what this secret file, which was locked, might reveal.

This confession I was needing to read took me back to the church in Hoogstraten and the confessional that I found myself in. As I shared earlier, I was taught about the scripture to confess your sins one to another, and the truth shall set you free. Well, I had a secret sin that I knew I must confess to my husband for three reasons. One, so I could confess so I could be forgiven and set free; two, so he could confess and be forgiven and set free; and three, so he and I both could be forgiven and set free by the Lord so we could be what Christ wants husband and wife to be to one another! I knew we were far from being that!

Well, that was a far cry from the way it turned out. I confessed to my husband that many years ago, when he had asked for the legal separation, I had an affair. I explained the affair was for a short time, but the affair was what I felt I needed to get back my sense of worth that he had stripped me of. If you have never been in my shoes, you may not understand the sense of devastation I felt. I had given up everything and everybody just to be with him, and I felt he threw me away like a piece of garbage. I felt betrayed and ashamed of everyone and about every one of my actions that had caused me to be married to him.

My Christian husband didn't understand and didn't forgive me, no matter how hard I tried to make him understand or forgive me. I explained how I felt thrown away, how I felt he had thrown me away and moved into an apartment with another guy and threw wild parties and then even showed me a beautiful blonde he worked with and told me he had gone to her house while I was gone. To me, he was showing me a conquest... I was just supposed to be okay with the fact that he asked me to come back, and so everything was supposed to just be bliss, and the hurt I felt was just supposed to be gone.

The first time the man I had the affair with and I were together, he allowed me to not go any further than my panties because I began to cry. He asked why I was crying, and I told him what had happened with my husband and why I was actually doing this, and he let me get dressed, and nothing happened. He seemed to actually care, but he was persistent, so we were together twice after that. I needed reassurance from someone that I was worthy and that I was desirable. This man gave me that back, and that was really all I was seeking! I didn't need or want the man, only the belief in myself that he gave me back. He said he wanted to take me everywhere and show me off. He said he wanted to take me to the park, but at the same time, he also shared that he was married and showed me a picture of his two little girls. I told him this had to be the last time we would see each other when I found that out, which made it easier to do. Just because my husband asked me to come back didn't mean that my sense of self-worth came back at the same time. I still felt as undesirable to him as he had made me feel when he told me all the hurtful things, helped me pack, and watched me drive away. My confidence took a serious blow, and I don't think that without hearing it from someone else, I would have ever felt worthy of being with him. I could never seem to make my husband understand that, and therefore, he felt I never wanted or was seeking his forgiveness or that I had any guilt. Therefore, he commenced to convince me that I was the "devil herself."

So, as I expected he would, he then shared his confession with me. As a result of my confession to him, which I knew would have to be the bargaining chip, I was able to find out what his confession was. Although I wasn't pleased with the way things turned out with my confession, I still held out hope. Hope that once he shared, we could still be healed.

Well, my hopes and prayers were far, far, far from what happened. His confession turned out to be something as devastating and unbelievable to me as my confession was to him. His confession, however, was based on his childhood from the time he was seven. He confessed that he was a victim, and he became a predator, of child sexual abuse. There were four siblings involved from his description, two sisters and two brothers. But after a conversation with one of his brothers, who my husband didn't include, he informed me that he was also involved. To my understanding, an older brother was involved with his younger sister, who then was involved with the two younger brothers. My husband was then involved with a younger sister, which began when she was several years younger than him. Well, you can only imagine how utterly shocked I was by this confession.

But, with this confession, it explained a lot of his behaviors I had lived with and tried to figure out for twenty-three years now. There were many times when he would threaten to drive himself into a tree, and I would ask why... what was so wrong? There were many times when I would notice that he would not make eye contact when talking to others; he would look at me when telling a story to them that I had heard many times. He had a lot of unexplained anger and rage. A lot of anger was also towards his younger sister. He was always thinking he had some kind of deadly disease and said he was going to die when he hadn't even seen a doctor. I can recall him bragging, many times, about his older sister's figure measurements, and I always thought that was strange. There were signs of a sexual addiction early in our marriage, and it also explained his thirst for any and all sexual books and knowledge at such an early age.

Nevertheless, I prayed for a divine healing for both of us as well as our relationship. I had so much empathy for him, considering what he had gone through as a child, but I also wondered how he could have carried out the things he did with his sister when he was eleven. I felt he should have known better by then.

On the other hand, he had no empathy for me. I was inundated, over a period of about six months, by him, with about seventy-five pages of hand-typed mind-boggling letters, ten altogether, explaining how I had ruined his whole entire world and everything he thought he could believe in… in this life… me! And now, twenty-something years later, I share with him that I have committed this horrible sin against him!

I want to take you back now to chapter five. Remember the picturesque church I visited in Hoogstraten, Belgium, with the confessional. Well, of course, I confessed the adultery, along with the ten cents that I took out of someone's desk in the fourth grade, I think, along with some shampoo I took while working for a grocery because I didn't have the money to pay for it, and the dreaded white swimsuit I took from a store because I wanted it so bad but didn't have the money. I also wanted that swimsuit to impress my husband, which ironically wasn't long after he asked me to leave, and I came back. Others had told me how easy it was to put it on under your clothes and walk out with it on. It is amazing the thoughts that other people can put in your mind, that it may work on your young mind to the point that you rationalize it, even though you know better. You can reject your own morals when tempted.

That being said, I understood how both of us committed the sins we had done! After all, we were like Jesus and lived in the

flesh, and He, too, was tempted! We have fleshly desires and
wants, and Satan knows how to tempt us all!

So, I was fervently in prayer! I continued to go to church and seek guidance and protection while my husband, on the other hand, sought whatever he needed in pool halls and bars… but couldn't seem to understand why I asked him to find a different place to live. He insisted we needed to heal each other and work this out while he drowned his sorrows with alcohol, bars, and drugs again! I was still praying for a divine intervention all the while this was happening, but I explained to him that if we were to heal that we needed time apart because what he was doing was not healing either of us or especially not good for the children.

Before this happened, he had planned a wonderful vacation for us, from his perspective, to fix everything. However, he had stayed out all night the night before, and even though we had planned on leaving around 5 a.m. for the long drive, he wasn't home. I was just about to leave with the children alone for this wonderful vacation he had planned, which was already paid for, and he showed up around 7 a.m. He expected, because he was then present, for all to be well and good and for us to be happy and harmonious. We took the trip, but it was not at all the happy, harmonious venture he had planned. Of course, with him being out all night, and it was apparent to me he had taken something, he was in no shape to drive, and our safety was in jeopardy because of it. I had to insist on driving… much to his disagreement. I can also remember being in the hot tub playing with the kids, and I could see him at the bar making great friends with someone instead of being with us, which was usual and customary.

It was a beautiful setting at Clearwater Beach Resort.
But only the water was clear… nothing else was!

True Confessions

True confessions are ones that are shared from the heart,
True confessions are shared so they can be cleansed from your
   heart!
True confessions aren't shared to be used as guilt,
True confessions are shared so you can be cleansed from the
   guilt!

We have all sinned, and it is not for us to compare,
Or Satan will keep us in his deadly snare!
Unless we forgive each other of our ugly sins,
Only Satan will rejoice because he knows that he wins!

As it says in the Bible, we must forgive one another,
If we wish to be forgiven by our heavenly Father!
For our Father doesn't measure one sin to the other,
To sin against one, is to sin to the Father!

For there is only one unforgivable sin,
It's not to believe, profess and proclaim!
That you believe in the Father and call out His name!
And then He will bless and forgive us all,
And we can know that to Him, we can always call!

Just call out His name and believe with your heart,
That He has forgiven you, and from you, He will never part!
Though life may be tough in the days and roads ahead!
But you will be born again, and the old you will be dead!

No matter the sin or the injustices you've done,
With Jesus in your heart… you have most definitely won!
Amen!

Written on October 3, 2015, at 4:28 p.m.
Thank You, Lord, for forgiveness! Amen!

CHAPTER 7

Seeking a Healing

1997–1998

It was February 1997 when we both shared our confessions with one another. As a result of my confession, as I mentioned earlier, I was inundated with a lot of paperwork from my husband. As I mentioned earlier, it was mind-boggling information. There are eleven documents between us.

1. His confession to me is eleven pages of typed information.

2. A half-page handwritten request from me to him asking for a copy of his confession along with a letter he had given me the night before that upset me so much, after reading the first paragraph, that I gave it back to him. He responded to this with a page of insults to me.

3. Although he responded with insults, he gave me his ten-page (typed) "Letter of Love to My Darling Trish," which in no way resembled love or forgiveness, only condemnation. I called my mentor at 5 a.m. in the morning and asked if I could come over because I desperately needed someone to talk to and read what I had been given because I needed some advice and some sanity.

4. A one-page letter from my husband to the man I had an affair with, in which he acted as though he were me and I was desperately looking for and wanting to reunite with this man. He sent this to several newspapers. He put a

PO Box on there that I was unaware of. I questioned, and he admitted that he had had this for a long time and had been ordering pornography.

5. A six-page typed letter from my husband to me where he asked me to remarry him and then commenced to ask me five pages of unrealistic questions about the affair and very specific and sick questions about the relations we had, which stemmed from his pornography videos, no doubt.

6. A one-page typed apology from my husband for being so blunt in his "Tough Love" letter.

7. A thirteen-page handwritten letter from me to him about mine and his entire relationship and the problems we had in addition to our confessions.

8. A two-page typed letter from him telling me how he felt about my letter. Still not understanding how or why I did what I did.

9. A three-page typed "Custom Mephisto Ideas" letter from my husband to me, which is a subconscious tape letter which is as the first line reads, "Sharing intimate passion with 'name' is a blessing."

10. A one-page typed Surveys Questionnaire Checklist, which he made for me to answer about him. I told him I wouldn't answer it unless he did. Of course, he came up with the questions for us both, and they were different, of course.

11. A twenty-four page, which is more like forty-four because of the font, journal which was my husband's thoughts, emotions, and obsessions of my confession. The first line says, "I will not give you a complete copy because it's now beyond fifty pages, and parts of it would only make you

resent me more than you already do!" So, the fifty pages would be more like one hundred pages.

You are probably wondering why I have kept all this almost twenty years later. Well, I will have to tell you what happened as a result of all this for you to understand why and how I have kept this.

Because of the tragedy and trauma our confessions caused, we sought counseling. First, we visited our pastor but not before my husband sent him a letter to explain to him that we needed help because I was a controlling wife. That, according to my husband, was supposed to be the reason for our counseling. Also, I wasn't privy to this letter he had sent and was unaware of it until our visit. You can imagine my surprise when it was mentioned by the pastor. I, however, was unwilling to play games and was ready to lay things on the table. No matter how ugly things were, for both of us. I was tired of the battle but knew the only way the battle would be won was to be open and honest and get both guidance and prayer for us to be healed.

Well, I was very glad that the preacher spoke up when my husband complained that I wanted him to put his clothes in the hamper instead of on the lid. The preacher asked if he had ever washed a load of clothes. He hesitated and said, "Well, I work." The preacher advised him that he did too, but he did all the clothes and vacuuming at his house. My husband commenced to tell him I fussed at him if he didn't put the lid back on the toothpaste. The preacher said, "My son does that, and it makes me mad too. If you can open it, you can close it." I explained all because I had seen a documentary about roaches liking toothpaste and had simply asked. I even went so far as to plant a rubber roach to make the point; no point was made, but I was however instructed to buy him the new pop-top toothpaste now. He, of course, didn't go any further after the preacher didn't side with him on the two issues he brought to the table to prove my control. I'm sure he would have shared that I expected him to fill all the ice trays after he emptied them and threw them on top of the refrigerator for tennis instead of fussing at me if they were still sitting there empty the next day when he needed them for tennis again. Or I would ask him to file all his papers away in the filing cabinet I bought him instead of yelling at me if he couldn't find a paper he had laid down a year ago. Or that I asked him to trim his mustache or his beard into a towel and empty it instead of leaving it all over the sink for me to clean up. He wouldn't dare now share that we had been going back and forth with a towel full of beard and mustache hair that he had placed at the back door on the floor instead of emptying it. After about a month of putting it on top of his clothes in the closet every day to find it back on the floor at the back door, I finally gave in and emptied it.

You see, after so many years of being expected to do everything and getting no appreciation in return, I knew from the Bible that the Lord wanted more for us! I was not supposed to be a submissive wife, as he highlighted and finger-pointed to me on a regular basis, but I was supposed to be a mate, a partner. I was supposed to be loved by my husband the way the Lord loves the church. I wasn't feeling loved; I was feeling used and abused.

I grew up in a household where my Diddy had just nodded or pointed if he wanted a refill of coffee. I grew up in a household where my Mama clipped my Diddy's toenails. I grew up in a household where someone else, myself included, polished my Diddy's shoes. I grew up in a household where women did all the household chores. I grew up in a household where children were spoken to but never should be heard unless spoken to.

I grew up, in other words, to be a very submissive person. I had been a very submissive wife. I had done everything for my husband to make his life better. I did, however, try to stand up for myself and not become a doormat. He, on the other hand, expected me to engage with him every night even though I was given nothing all day to enhance that desire.

The knowledge he gained from the Bible, on the other hand, allowed him to not only expect but demand. He demanded me to be submissive to him. As he described in one section of his many letters to me, my body was not my own, and he was not to be deprived. He, however, failed to realize that he was not treating me the way the Lord desired for him to treat me in order for me to want to give up my body to him and not deprive him. For many years I had tried to talk to him, and he would always get angry whenever I mentioned our sex life or the lack of birth control. So, for many years unless I just did it anyway, we had no formal means of birth control. It was against his will and God's too, as he would insist to me, even before us being saved.

We had our second session with the pastor, who had asked the music minister to also attend. I don't remember how much of the actual true situation was shared at the first visit, but I was still praying for a divine healing and knew it wasn't going to happen without some outside help.

On the morning we were supposed to go for counseling, I miraculously found a book that I didn't know was in my home and was shocked at not only how I found it but what it contained. I was led to find this book which had been hidden under a one-inch shelf that was on my side of our closet. We both had a side, mine on one side, his on the other. Well, I ran my hand under my side of the one-inch gap to the floor and found a three-fourths-inch book. The book was all about anal sex. I said nothing, but I had a big purse that I took with me to counseling. I didn't know how or when this would be brought out, but I knew it had to be. As I found it, I assumed I had found some more of the sickness that my husband was living with that had him in so much turmoil, and that also caused his unwillingness to forgive because he couldn't forgive himself.

So, as we were counseling, and both of our confessions were brought out, I had asked the pastor if I was wrong in asking my husband if he had ever bothered our own children, considering his past.

The pastor agreed that was a valid concern and asked my husband if he would answer me. He answered that he had not, although I shared that he had walked around in our home naked even as recently as our first counseling session, even though I had asked him for years to stop. The pastor advised him to discontinue that behavior. I pulled the book out and gave it to the pastor and told him I had found it in my home and didn't know it was there and didn't want it there anymore. He asked my husband if it was his and if he minded if he kept it. Of course, he let him keep it. We were instructed by the pastor to visit a licensed professional counselor.

Our first visit to her was together. My husband said everything I had wanted to hear for years. He admitted he had been wrong; he admitted he had been a workaholic, an alcoholic, and a drug addict. He admitted he was manic-depressive. He admitted he had threatened to run himself into a tree many times. He said that he put me on a pedestal. I felt the pedestal had to be on the floor. But his version of the pedestal he put me on was I was awesome. He was proud that I was his wife, and he loved me dearly.

I admitted things to the counselor, and we left. As we were leaving, I thought we might be making progress. As we got in the car, he looked at me and growled, "You have always tried to change me, and I ain't changing." Well, right then and there was my turning point. Our next session with this counselor was supposed to be separate visits. I told her what happened when we got in the car, and I inundated the counselor with all the paperwork I described earlier. I told her if she wanted to truly know what was going on in this relationship, she needed to read all of it. On my next visit, she asked me if I was familiar with bipolar; I explained that he had advised me he was manic-depressive and now in addition something called a voyeur as he had explained to me was someone who likes to see others either disrobing or in a sexual act. She commenced to explain all the above to me and advised I needed help with dealing with his rage and advised me that we needed to go to a psychiatrist.

Well, I was tired, and I was both mentally and physically exhausted, but I repeated the same with the psychiatrist and inundated him with the paperwork after our initial visit. Our visits were separate, but he went in first, and then I went in. When I came out to the car, he asked me what the psychiatrist had prescribed me. I told him that he didn't give me anything. He insisted that he meant to give me a prescription and insisted we both go back in for it. He even insisted they interrupt the psychiatrist, who was already on his next visit, so we could have my prescription. The psychiatrist himself had to convince my husband that I didn't need anything.

On my next visit with the psychiatrist, I was advised that my husband needed extensive counseling. I was advised that he would be placed in group therapy and that he had a personality disorder. I was advised that he may not be able to help him. I was advised that my husband might never be okay. I was advised that in order for him to participate in group therapy, I would have to come at least once a month, or else my husband probably wouldn't come.

So, I conceded to a once-a-month visit, which consisted of me sharing what was happening with my husband and how my husband said everyone in the group meetings was crazy but him, and he didn't understand why he was in them. This went on for a while, along with all the rambling conversations from my husband. He had moved into an apartment when I asked him to leave and was running credit cards up like crazy, buying himself all new furnishings, a van identical to the one I had but nicer, staying in bars all the time, but still trying to convince me that we needed to be back together. I had to make the decision to go back into this world I hated, which I believed would be even darker and bleaker considering everything that had happened.

I called between one of my scheduled monthly visits and advised the psychiatrist that I was asking for a divorce. I was advised by the psychiatrist that my husband was addicted to two things, sex and me, and that he could not guarantee me that my husband wouldn't try to kill me. I felt I had to take that chance not only for myself but also for my children. I truly believed that the Lord would not allow anything to happen to me. I put my trust in Him. I had been in a lot of prayers over this the entire time.

We were officially divorced in July 1998…

So back to the question earlier as to why I have kept this all these years: I felt if my husband was ever going to truly get the help he needed, if he ever realized he needed it, whoever was supposed to help him would need this information in order to give him the help he needed and deserved. He has been institutionally committed several times recently but still didn't and doesn't realize the need.

Not only had I been in a lot of prayers, but I had spent a lot of time studying the Bible before I had the peace to make the hardest decision of not only my life but also my children's lives as well.

> *During this time, I had an experience, I felt, that I described to both the pastor and my mentor as a* **"spiritual cleansing."**

In the early hours of the morning, I woke and was burning from the inside out. It wasn't a fever. I just felt a warmth from inside that was indescribable, although I tried to describe it. When I called to describe and ask my pastor if there was anything in the Bible that resembled what I was describing, he told me I must just have a fever. I told him it was not a fever; it was a burning, which to me felt like a cleansing inside of my being.

When I shared this with my mentor, she was quick to reference scripture to validate my description of what I felt and believed had happened to me, which was a spiritual cleansing.

There is scripture, in Psalm 39:3 (NIV), "My heart grew hot within me, and as I meditated, the fire burned; then I spoke with my tongue."

Also, in Luke 24:32 (NIV), "They asked each other, 'Didn't our hearts feel strangely warm as he talked with us on the road and explained the Scriptures to us?'" One may think I'm crazy, and if you have never felt what I felt, you probably may think so. But I believe the same Lord that spoke to David and the disciples is the same Lord we serve today, and He is still alive today! If He could speak to people then, I believe He can speak to people today! Whatever He did then, He can do now! We just have to have the faith of a mustard seed, and anything is possible.

I, however, had to realize that even though the Lord can do any-thing, He must have a willing participant. My husband was not willing to forgive me. His plan, on the other hand, with all his paperwork, was to make me more like who he wanted me to be. I didn't want to be an object for him. I wanted us to have a mutual objective. It was very plain to me and, thank God, for my mentor that he had an agenda that was not what the Lord would have us be together. My mentor was there for me and, quite honestly, the only thing that kept me sane at the time besides the Lord and the Bible.

A Spiritual Cleansing

As I lay on the couch early one morn,
I discussed my life with the Lord and told Him how I was
    torn,
I felt a burning from deep inside,
It was so moving I could not hide!

I could not hide the joy that I felt,
I lay there in the night, and with Jesus I wept,
I knew beyond a shadow of doubt that He came to me,
To cleanse the hurt and pain that only He could see!

He knew what I felt and what I needed from Him,
Although I didn't know what it was, I knew it wasn't a
whim,
The warmth I felt was a cleansing deep inside,
For only He knew all the things that I had held inside!

So, with this cleansing became a new awakening,
And I knew that what I was being dealt I was no longer
taking,
For the Lord of all lords is a lover indeed,
He came and loved me and fulfilled a deep need!

A need to be cleansed from all the hurt and pain!
That was being inflicted on me from someone who says they
love me by name,
But actions speak a whole lot louder than words,
And the Lord let me know that He also heard!

He heard the cries that I shed in the night,
He heard the pleas that I cried in my fright,
He answered them all as I lay there in pain,
Now I had to decide if I win, lose, or gain!

All the things that this spiritual cleansing offered to me,
I was the only one that could truly see,
So, I made the decision to move ahead,
It's a decision that I never did dread!
Amen!

Written on October 4, 2015, at 6:27 a.m.
Thank You, Lord, for what you have done for me!

CHAPTER 8
An Awesome Journey

1997

In the midst of all the turmoil going on with my husband in 1997, I was approached by a gentleman after church one day after getting up and making a bold yet powerful statement to the church that morning that he needed to talk to me. He was a married man, who rode a Harley Davidson and even wore his jeans and chaps to church sometimes, and we always had a good greeting during fellowship, and I knew his wife from the doctor's office I had worked at. They hadn't been married long, and I was as happy for them as she was. Well, he asked me if I would like to go do prison ministry. He explained that the ministry was a Bill Glass—who used to be a famous pro football player—Prison Ministry, and they go in prisons with their motorcycles. I was quick to advise him that I couldn't go into men's prisons. He explained to me that I would be going into women's prison. I said, "Oh, okay then."

So, I signed up to go to Perry, Georgia. It was explained that people came from all over to do this, and everyone pays their own way. I immediately decided that if people are willing to pay their own way, it's got to be awesome. Well, awesome is an understatement!

There were over 500 counselors, and a local church was our meeting place, and they fed us both breakfast and dinner.

The first year I went, as I said, I was also dealing with the turmoil with my husband, but I was already cleansed and on my way to recovery and beyond! I took a friend with me. She was a dear, precious, beautiful person inside and *out*. Unfortunately, most people never got past her looks to find that out. You see, she had what you may know as "elephant man's disease" from the movie *Elephant Man*. The tumors consumed one side of her face, and therefore, the other side was drawn too. It also affected her speech, but she was able to pronounce her words well, but it worked better if you looked at her as she spoke, and for most people, even in the church we went to, that was hard to do.

She and I had become close at church, and she actually shared how she had been hurt by some not giving her the time of day and obviously avoiding her. She also shared with me her entire life of hurt and being made fun of and abused by her husband. But to me, she was beautiful and even more beautiful than most.

I got to know her from the inside out instead of the outside in!

She could write beautiful poetry, and I still have some of the poems she wrote for me. Even though she had little, she always wanted to give me something. If that doesn't make one feel humble, nothing will. One of my favorite things she gave me is in my office today. Just a little four-by-five-inch glossy note that says, "Be careful, or I'll include you in my plans." On the back, it says, "Count on it." I was proud to be her friend and proud to be included in her plans.

So, I took her with me on my first trip to the prison ministry. On the way there, she taught me a song she had written. So, when we got to the prison after our training, she and I went in and met about five girls, and we struck up a conversation, and then we sang her song for them. They were enjoying, swaying, clapping, and moving to the song. Those five girls quickly became about thirty. When we finished, I told the girls they sure were getting into our song. They told me it was like one they sang there. I jokingly said, "Well, maybe we can sing it for everyone since y'all like it so much." They told me that we should. Well, there was a flatbed trailer that was brought in as the stage. There were famous people who were supposed to be there giving their testimonies.

There were wrestlers, football players, famous musician's wives, Miss Georgia, and a man who had received a pardon for stealing the world's largest diamond. Well, naïve loudmouth me walked up to the person in charge of those events and told her about my friend and I singing and them telling us we should sing it for everybody. She told me to get on stage. I was shocked and asked, "Are you kidding?" And she said, "No." She said that Miss Georgia was supposed to be there and didn't show. So, my friend and I went up on stage and sang her song with thousands of prisoners sitting out there yelling and screaming and clapping and cheering. Wow! My friend and I took Miss Georgia's place. What a blessing, and I was thinking about what a beautiful replacement my friend made for Miss Georgia! She was so blessed on the way home she just lay in the back seat of my van, while I drove, and reminisced about how awesome the trip was. I was blessed for many reasons, but I was also blessed that she was so blessed!

Well, with this singing adventure we had, it gave her a sense of confidence that she was okay with us not staying together and going off on our own. So, the first thing I decided was that I was going to be bold like my pastor had been preaching. You see, I decided my time there was short, and I didn't want to waste it by talking to someone that really didn't want to hear what I was there to share, Jesus! I decided that since they knew in advance that we were coming and what we were coming for, I would just ask if they wanted to talk to me.

So, up in the path in front of me, I see three young black girls heading toward me. I said, "You know what I am here for, and if you want to talk to me, we can talk, but if not, I will move along."

Well, the young girl in the middle began to talk. She shared with me that she was saved, but she also explained, "It is hard in here."

Well, as I said earlier, I had decided to be bold. So, it was apparent to me this girl had a rough life. So, I asked, "What happened to your face? How did you get all the cuts?" You see, she had about seventeen knife cuts all over her face.

She explained, "My boyfriend got a hold of me." I believe that was the way she put it.

I began to share with her about my life. The other two girls that were with her had already slipped away from our conversation. We shared with one another, and she said something to me that I was somewhat perplexed about, but at the same time, I knew she was giving me a compliment, but I wasn't exactly sure what it meant. She told me that I was a prophet! Wow! I was such a new Christian that I really didn't know what that meant… but I knew it was good. She explained that she knew I was because I was telling her everything she needed to hear. She told me she knew another prophet once, and she did the same thing. Well, we were well on our way to a great conversation when the sound alarm that we had been trained that no matter what you are doing or in the middle of when we heard, we were supposed to drop everything and leave quickly because they had a regimen to follow. So, begrudgingly, I left as instructed.

I was so pleased when we were allowed back in… my dear friend with the cuts found me! She came looking for me and said she wanted to talk to me some more. We sat down on a huge, paved area along with several other groups and counselors. But in our group, it was she and I. We talked and shared for a while, and then she asked me a question that made me say to myself, *Wow, that's deep; how do I answer that?* She asked, "How do you know you have the Holy Spirit?"

As I said, my first reaction was, "Wow, that's deep," and my second was, "How do I answer that?" It seemed as though time had stopped, and I looked out and saw the trees and the wind and the words, and the thoughts to answer this most powerful question just came from me; they came from a knowledge that I didn't have, and I knew it as soon as I said it. It was too beautiful of an analogy to come from me. I said, "Well, it is kinda like the wind; sometimes you can see it, sometimes you can't, sometimes you can feel it, sometimes you can't, but it's always there. It's kinda like a cold chill going down your spine."

She said, "Well, that's happening right now."

I said, "Well, that's the Holy Spirit!" We continued to minister to one another as she was as much a blessing to me as I was to her. You see, she had shared her sorrows with me, and I shared my sorrows with her. We both had pain, but we both also had gain. We rejoiced together that even though we had both been through trials and tribulations that the Lord was still Lord, and He still loved us both and wanted to, and showed His love to us in an awe-inspiring way, in prison!

It wasn't until two weeks later that I even knew that the wind and the Holy Spirit were compared to one another in the Bible.

I shared in Sunday school the beautiful analogy that came from me.

The pastor told me it was in the Bible. Wow—confirmation!

Just as you can hear the wind but can't tell where it comes from or where it is going, so you can't explain how people are born of the Spirit.

—John 3:8, NLT

Well, the blessings didn't end with the previous encounter I just shared. There was another beautiful situation that happened. There was a speaker on stage; I believe it was Jack Roland Murphy, who was pardoned for stealing the world's largest diamond. I had a group of girls sitting beside me on the curb. The girl sitting next to me, who I could sense had a sweet spirit, but I hadn't talked to, whispered to me and asked me what I had in the clear pouch on my side. I explained to her that it was information that they could fill out to have stuff sent to them after we were gone. She shared with the girl next to her, who shared with the girl next to her until all knew what I had and sent word back that they wanted one. I passed them out, and all the girls, probably fifteen to twenty, had one, and she gave me hers back. I whispered, as we were taught to set the example and be quiet when there was a speaker, "You don't want one?"

She said, "No."

I whispered, "You sure you don't want one?"

She said, "No," and shook her head again.

I just prayed and asked the Lord what it was. My prayer was answered that she couldn't read. As I got this answer, she got up to walk away. I whispered, "Ha," real loud, and when she turned, I told her I wanted to talk to her when this was over. When the testimony was over, she came jolly bopping up to me and asked what I wanted to talk to her about. I said, "I know why you don't want the brochure."

She said, "You do?"

I said, "Yes... the Lord told me you can't read."

Her eyes got very big, and she took a step back and said, "He did?"

I said, "Yes, He did."

She said as she took another step back, "He did?"

I explained to her that she didn't have to know how to read to have Jesus and that He would send her what and who she needed.

She said again, "He did?"

I explained that she could take the brochure and get stuff, and the Lord would send her someone to read it or to do what she needed. Well, here came the horrible sound again that made me drop what I was doing and leave. It was hard, but I walked away. But I also left knowing that if I never saw her again that I was used to plant a seed, and the Lord would do the rest!

When we were allowed to come back, a famous musician's wife was giving her testimony, and it was very powerful and emotional. At the end of her testimony, the counselors were asked to form circles with those who wanted to give their lives to the Lord. So, I was in a circle with a couple of other counselors and about thirty girls saying the sinner's prayer. As the prayers were finished, I opened my eyes, and the girl standing the closest to me was a young black girl who had a tattoo of a cross between her eyes. I asked her if she wasn't saved prior to that moment, why she had the cross tattooed on her forehead. She shrugged and said she didn't know. I said, "Well, you know why it is there now." I also told her to never forget why it was there because I told her the devil will try to make you believe you didn't get what you just got. But I said, "That cross should be a daily reminder to you that you did and don't ever think anything different." I said, "The devil will be strongly after you trying to make you think you didn't get what you just got, but don't you ever believe it." I also told her that, to me, that's one of the most important things for a new Christian to hear and know because it is true.

Well, the next day was Sunday, and all we were there for was church, and then we were leaving. They were doing church for us. Well, my newfound "cross girlfriend" found me and said she wanted to go to church with me! What an honor! She and I stood side by side and sang and clapped and swayed our love for the Lord and each other. Before long, my other newfound "cuts girlfriend" found me too, and all three of us rejoiced and praised the Lord together!

When church was over, and I was in the bathroom, another counselor said that a girl was looking for me. I asked, "Did she have a gold tooth?" The answer was yes, so I knew that my newfound "couldn't read girlfriend" was looking for me. I was okay because I knew the Lord would finish the work that He allowed me to start! Amen

Wonderful Things Happen... Even in Prison Too

Wonderful things happen, even in prison too,
If you are willing to just let the Lord use you!

Those beautiful girls that I met in this place,
I know one day I will, again, get to see their face!

For the blessings that the four of us shared,
Were also witnessed by the man upstairs!

Although I know none of them by name,
When we meet again, the feeling will be the same!

For the love and the bond that we shared,
Can't be replaced or be compared!

Each one was special to me in a different way,
And I honestly can't wait for that wonderful day!

That wonderful day that we get to meet again,
And I will know each by name, but most importantly as a
  friend!

Whether we get to meet in heaven or here on earth,
We can rejoice and share about our new birth!

Wonderful things happen, even in Prison too,
If you are willing to just let the Lord use you!
Amen!

Written on October 7, 2015, at 7:46 p.m.

Written especially for my three beautiful friends that I don't know
by name… only as my friends! Until we meet again!

CHAPTER 9

A Lonely Walk

1998–2006: Ages Forty-Two Through Fifty

I had taken the children, who were now thirteen, ten, and three, and rented a house in town, and I gave my husband the option of keeping or selling our house. I knew that I couldn't afford the $1500 per month just for the first and second mortgage and electricity on my $7 per hour wage, and I didn't think I would be able to count on him, although he was making $80K.

Unfortunately, I was right about not being able to count on him, and my lawyer had not seen fit to ensure that the child support that he agreed to pay me at mediation was set up to come through child support, so I never knew when or if I would get the child support money. Imagine trying to live off $7 per hour with a $500 monthly rent and three children. So, he used that as a way to stay in touch with me and ensure that I needed him.

I got stuck at Walmart one evening when my van wouldn't crank as I tried to leave. I didn't know what I was going to do because I knew I had no money. Luckily, someone I went to church with came out and was parked diagonally to me and gave my youngest daughter and me a ride home. I tried to call my mentor to see if her husband was available and willing to go see if he could find out what was wrong. I called a few other people, and there was no answer. I saw the man outside that I was renting from when I came around the corner with the people who brought me home.

I hated to bother him, but I didn't know what else to do. So, my daughter and I walked back down to his house and asked if he would help. He took us to Walmart and found that the battery terminal was corroded. He cleaned it and jumped the car off, and got me home. But the next morning, the car wouldn't start again, and he came and took the battery out and found that I needed a new battery. I had to call my husband, who had not paid the child support, so I could get another battery. He was angry to find that I had gotten help from another man. I told him that I didn't have a choice and that if he had given the child support like he was supposed to, I wouldn't have to be asking him for help.

I am sharing this so you will know that even though we were divorced, he still wanted to be in the midst of my comings, goings, and doings...

Although it was very scary to be forty-two, making $7 an hour, and having three children, I was strong... or pretending to be. I was driven and motivated to make it. Fortunately, the doctor I worked for offered to let me borrow the money for the divorce, or I don't know how I would have done it. With me making $7 an hour, $2500 was a lot to borrow and pay back, but I had faith that I could somehow do it, which I did. Looking back, I don't know how I did it, but I made a payment to him every time I was paid until the debt was gone. I worked for him for five years. It was a job I needed at the time because of all the stress I was under. It was a very easy job with little stress. The girls I worked with were shocked to find that I had divorced, and they didn't even know anything was going on.

It was about six months after our divorce, and he invited himself to my home only to find that there was another man inside with us, as he described when he looked through the window.

You see, my thirteen-year-old daughter had told me on two differ-ent occasions that the man I was renting from liked me. I was oblivious to what she saw, I guess, because I wasn't interested in a relationship.

But because of her prodding, I had come home from church one day and said a prayer as my three-year-old took off her dress and got on her tricycle and was riding in the driveway. I asked the Lord if what my daughter thought was true and if it was his will to send him by. Well, about five minutes later, he drove by, and I said, "Well, maybe so." He drove around the block and back up the street and pulled in, and I said, "Well, that's a definite 'yes.'" He had been stopping by if he saw me on the front porch, and we would talk prior to that, but I just thought he was being nice, nothing else.

So, it was a few months after that we began to date. I didn't really know much about him, but I was told by one of the ladies at work that he was very wealthy. I didn't know because I wasn't from this town, and you wouldn't know that by what he wore or necessarily what he drove. He also had a very old beat-up work truck. But as we dated, I did find that what my coworker said was true. He explained that his goal had been to be a millionaire by the time he was fifty. He had a huge home, and the first time I was there, I was amazed, but one of the most amazing things was that I saw him straighten up the rug in the hallway with his foot as we entered the hallway. I was totally impressed because I had been used to someone who never even noticed if they made a mess. But he noticed the rug was crooked. Wow!

He explained early on in our relationship that what attracted him to me was what he saw in me when I came to him after moving in and asked if I could split the balance of $250 that I still owed him for the $500 deposit into two payments instead of one, as planned, because I needed and wanted to go do some prison ministry. Therefore, I had to pay my way and needed to pay $125 this time and $125 next time so I could go and pay for my gas and hotel. I also, at the same time, innocently shared with him some of the things that had happened the last time I went, and that was why I wanted to go again!

As I said earlier, he told me he saw something in me that he wanted. Well, we got engaged six months after we began dating, but then we dated for the next three years. During those three years, there were a lot of signs that I should have seen that made me step back... way back.

He had lots of things that I tried to help him with. He had found out that his oldest son wasn't actually his son a year after his birth. This son was now sixteen and lived with him, though, and he feared him finding out that he wasn't his father. He set up a recorder under his house so he could listen in on conversations between his son and his mom. He was forever going under the house and listening to the recordings. He also heard other conversations his son was having that a father shouldn't be listening to. I finally convinced him that if his son was going to find out that he would find out whether he was recording him or not and that it wasn't healthy for him to listen to his conversations.

He also had a younger son that was born out of wedlock that he didn't see much or have much to do with. He did, however, have daily yelling conversations with that child's mom. I finally convinced him that if he wouldn't answer and argue back with her that she would stop calling because if he didn't give her the opportunity, then there would be no conversations or arguments. He paid her child support diligently even though he never actually got proof that he was the dad.

I also had to let him know early on in our relationship that he didn't have to buy me. He loved to go antique shopping. Anytime we went, he would ask me as we walked around if I saw anything I liked over and over again. I told him then and there, and later on, in the car, that I was not about money, and he didn't have to buy me anything, that I was with him because I wanted to be but not because of what he could buy me.

He was very involved with the son that lived with him and anything and everything he did or wanted. He was always taking him somewhere and wanted me to go with them and put my kids aside. He got so upset with me once when we were supposed to take his son somewhere, and my oldest daughter wanted me to take her and a friend to a modeling scout competition. Well, I decided I should take my daughter and had to tell him. He wasn't just mad; he was livid with me because I had told him that I would go before she asked me to take them. He was doing something similar for his son, and I couldn't believe he was so upset with me because I chose to support my daughter.

As you can see, everything to him centered around him and his, and I should have known better. We also had a wedding date set twice that came and went, and I should have known better. We eventually moved in together instead of marrying, and I should have known better. It lasted a week, and then he had a yelling episode with me because I moved something; I should have known better. I was told that "this was his palace."

So, I decided, then and there, that I was moving right back out of that "palace." He got very angry with me and yelled at me about what a fool I was making of him. My young fifteen-year-old son came to my defense because he was also in the kitchen when he lit in on me and asked him to let me speak, as I had tried many times, but to no avail. We moved out of his "palace" and his rental house, which I wasn't completely moved out of, and moved way across town into a house that I rented that didn't belong to him.

He came to me crying while I was moving out of his rental house, apologizing and telling me that he had gone to another church, not the one we had been going to, and got up and asked all of them to pray for him. I told him that was great, but after all that we had been through, and my kids had now gone through, we were moving into the house I had rented and already moved most of our stuff into. He asked if I needed help moving, and I said, "No." Later that day, his two sons came and brought my furniture.

So, he finished moving me, and then after about two months, he started calling me again and began coming by to see how I was doing. After a while, he asked how I was doing financially. Well, you can imagine the financial burden I was under just moving into a new place and having all the finances of moving along with monthly rent and deposits. By this time, I was probably making $9 per hour. I really didn't want his help, but I also didn't know how I was going to manage because I needed about $1,500 to get myself above drowning. At first, I told him I was fine, but he persisted and asked how I was paying for everything. I confessed that I was struggling. So, he offered to help me, and I felt I really didn't have a choice, so I accepted even though I should have known better. I just didn't understand how he could be so kind one minute and turn on you like a bull the next. His explanation for yelling and being upset at me was that he didn't feel right about us living together instead of marrying. So, about six months later, we married. We had our wedding in his palace. I came down from the upstairs, and my son met me at the bottom, walked me up, and gave me away in the formal living room in front of the fireplace.

The guests were only immediate family and a few friends, and they just stood in the living room and sunroom off the living room during the ceremony. My two daughters were in the wedding too, my oldest was my maid of honor, and my youngest was the flower girl. My sister and I did all the decorations and the food for the reception, which was also held in his formal dining room and kitchen while the guests meandered throughout the house. There were three bedrooms, each had a fireplace, a large formal living room with a fireplace, a midsized sunroom with a fireplace, a large formal dining room, a large kitchen with a fireplace, a large den with a fireplace, and one bath downstairs. There were three bedrooms, another large living room, and another bath upstairs. The entire house was decorated with antiques from top to bottom. He had totally gutted and remodeled the entire house, so it was trimmed out and painted beautifully with beautiful stained glassed doors, so quite a palace it was!

So, my son, youngest daughter, and I moved back into the palace with him and his oldest son while my oldest daughter continued college. Well, as you may have imagined, it was probably not easy for either of us. I wasn't from a background of wealth and having anything and everything I wanted, and neither were my kids. He and his kids were, however, very blessed and didn't know what it was like to wonder where or how you were going to get the money for maybe even a hamburger. As soon as we moved in, though, he had a discussion with me and informed me that he wanted $500 per month from me for the household. I agreed that I would give him $500 per month, although I found it strange that when I was renting his house, as soon as we were engaged, he refused to take the $500 rent from me. I insisted, but he refused, so I made a bargain that I would cook dinner every night, and he and his son would come and eat with us instead because I wasn't going to live in his house for free. So that is what we did for more than three years.

Well, this turned into a constant source of struggle. Struggle for me because I wouldn't have the $500 he wanted, and struggle for him to get it from me or fuss at me because I couldn't get it from my ex-husband. He was constantly fussing at me because he wasn't paying child support and constantly fussing at me to fuss at him to get it. I knew that I was fighting a losing battle from both sides. I explained to him I felt like I was in a tug of war and there was no way for me to win. By this time, I had two teenagers, one still in college and trying to make ends meet by working and going to school full time, and my son was in school and working full time at a restaurant. His son, on the other hand, went to school and worked for him after school and made about $300 per week but was always broke come Monday, and Dad would hand him money. Don't get me wrong; I didn't just move in and expect him to pay for everything. I did what I could when I could. When I had spare money, I would just go to the grocery and buy stuff to cook for all of us. I was always cooking homemade chili, homemade vegetable soup, lasagna, spaghetti, ham, pork chops and gravy, Ritz cracker chicken, and lots more stuff. I made several flower arrangements for the house. He also bought some from me because I had started making them when I had moved out to make extra money. Money, however, was tight for me because I would try to help my daughter in college if she called and told me she was broke and didn't have money for even the bare necessities. I had two teenagers driving, and the insurance alone was $500 a month, along with three car payments. I had gotten my son a $7,000 car, my daughter had a $7,000 car until she went to college, and I got her a leased Civic so she would have a good car since she was three hours away from me. He however bought his son a more than $20,000 truck but fussed at me when I got my son the $7,000 car and told me I couldn't afford it. I believe the worst he said to me about what I couldn't afford was that he said, "You can't even afford toilet paper."

So, here I am again in a relationship where I feel I was put there to help show this man the spirit of the Lord. After all, that is what he said attracted him to me. Unfortunately, that was a way tougher job than I was able to accomplish. No matter how I poured out my heart to him, and on paper, and tried to make him understand that it wasn't good for him to buy me a four-wheeler but then tell me that no one was allowed to ride it but me while he and his sons had everything including four wheelers to ride. I poured out my heart, and on paper, about a year into our marriage, explaining to him all the harmful and damaging things he was causing to our relationship. Unfortunately, nothing changed. It just continued to get worse.

You may wonder why I have expressed I poured my heart out and on paper. I have been told and learned that when you are in the presence of someone, they may not truly be listening. They are, instead, on the defense, and the best way to truly get through to someone is on paper because they must read it to themselves! Therefore, you aren't there in their presence for them to argue with, but they instead hear themselves reading it; therefore, it is heard better by them.

The breaking point came approximately three and a half years later. My youngest daughter, who was ten at the time, was hospitalized on Monday, and on Wednesday, they decided to do exploratory surgery on Thursday morning to find the root of her high fever and breast being very swollen and tender to touch. I had been in the hospital with her since Monday, and on Wednesday night at 10:50 p.m., I was awakened by my cell phone. I answered to an angry voice, which was my husband telling me that my son wasn't home. I asked what time it was, and he told me, and I said that his curfew was eleven and he was always home by eleven. I asked him to give him the other ten minutes. He responded to me by saying, "Get some g** d*** sleep, then," and hung up the phone on me.

I was hurt, first, that he would do that to me, knowing the stress I had been under and the fact that my baby was going down for exploratory surgery early the next morning, and him acting like this was the last thing I needed to be worried about. I was hurt, second, that he had such little respect for me or the Lord to use such language.

Nevertheless, I called my son and asked where he was. He told me he was at his best friend's house, which was not far. I asked if he could leave and go on home. He told me he would but asked why I was calling because he is always home on time. I told him my husband had just called upset with me, and I asked if he would let him know when he got there. He said since he was being a jerk, he wouldn't tell him anything. So, I lay there till around 11:30 p.m. and tried to call my son to make sure he had gotten there and everything was okay. His phone was dead, so he didn't answer, so I lay there worried, but of course, I didn't want to call my husband after the way he had acted. Finally, around 1:30 a.m., my son answered and told me everything was fine but that he didn't talk to my husband when he came in, and I understood why he wouldn't want to.

Early the next morning, they came and wheeled my daughter off. I went with her as far as I was allowed to go, kissed her goodbye, and told her the angels would be with her. She was ten, and it was very scary for her to know she was going to be put to sleep and cut on to find the problem. I left and went to the waiting room and began to cry and feel the loneliness that I shouldn't have had to feel. I, too, was scared and worried, not knowing what they would come back and tell me and if my daughter was going to live. I knew in my heart that if my husband really cared about my daughter or me the way he should, he would be there with me through the most difficult time in my life.

So, I decided since he had done what he had the night before that I would call him. I said to myself, I need to call him for two reasons. One reason was that he would probably be mad if I didn't, and the second reason was to see if he said he was coming. I decided before I made the call that if he asked me if I wanted him to come, instead of him knowing he should be there, my answer would be "no." Well, his response was exactly that. Do you want me to come because all I can do is come and sit there? With his response, as I said, my response was, "No, I'm fine." I felt so alone, upset, foolish, and heartbroken. His actions during this very trying and difficult time spoke volumes to me.

I called my mentor crying and told her what had happened and that I was alone and afraid. She, of course, came to my rescue and sat with both my daughter and me most of the day and read her stories once she came back from recovery. She was diagnosed with Methicillin-resistant Staphylococcus aureus (MRSA), which was a new type of staph infection that the CDC was investigating. They were trying to find the source as most staph infections are acquired in a hospital, and this was a community-acquired staph, and they still didn't know where the source was coming from. There were many deaths from MRSA as it was resistant to most antibiotics, and it took a while to find what worked.

I was so thankful my mentor was there with me when I got the diagnosis. It was so nice to know that someone truly cared and especially cared enough just to come and sit with us. She was, and is, such a good friend and mentor, and as I explained to her, she was like the mother I never had. Although I had a mother, we never talked for hours on the phone or met to have lunch or shared stories about our lives like we do. I'm sure I don't have to tell you how she felt about the situation I was in.

On Saturday, my daughter's father, my ex-husband of twenty-three years, had finally made it from Arkansas to see her. So, I left the hospital for the first time all week. Instead of going home, I went to the park first as I really wasn't looking forward to going home and, quite frankly, didn't know what I may walk into. I sat on a park bench and prayed and talked to the Lord about my situation. I was seeking His guidance and direction and wanted clarity from Him as to how to handle this heartbreaking situation. My plea to the Lord was to give me a peace as to whether I should stay in this relationship or go. I left the park and the bench two hours later, believing that I had His guidance and the peace to go. The problem was I knew I couldn't go now, so I asked Him to let me know when.

Well, as soon as I did go home, I got confirmation that what I believed when I left the park was right. You see, my oldest daughter was in college three hours away and hadn't been able to come home to be with us or see her sister. She had a rental car because she had wrecked her car, but she had picked her car up, and the rental was parked on the side of the road in front of "my husband's house," which was on a two-lane road leading north into town. My daughter and son had wanted to take the patient, their sister, a gift, but being short on money, they went to yard sales to find her some stuffed animals. They were just backing out of the driveway when he pulled up, and as I was motioning for them that they could back out because his truck was blocking their view, he abruptly told me to get them to take the rental back so he could clean up his yard. I ignored him and continued to motion to them to back out. Like I said earlier, I wasn't looking forward to coming home, and you can see why.

After they left, I went inside and asked if he would take me to take the car back, and he responded, "H*** no," that he had told me to get them to. So, I took the car back myself and decided I would walk the mile or two back. The place I had to take the car to was not in the best part of town, but I was so mad I didn't care. A few blocks into my walk, a kind black man stopped and asked if I needed a ride. I responded and told him that I just lived a short distance down the road and told him my husband was being a jerk and I needed to walk. Now you must understand for me to blow off steam like that to a stranger was way out of my behavior pattern, but one can only take so much, and I had had it!

So, I am about a half mile from home, and I see his truck coming down the two-lane road coming south out of town. I am almost to the section where you can turn from South Center Street to go back North Center Street, and he pulls into the turn and sits there waiting on me. I walk up to the truck, and he lets down the window and tells me to get in. I told him I was not getting in that truck.

He said, "We need to talk."

I said, "You're d*** right we need to talk, but right now, I need to walk, and you can just go because I will not be getting in that truck." I had never stood up to him like that, even let anger show until now, but it was past time for me to stand up and be heard and listened to. So, when I got home, he was inside. I went in and told him I wanted to talk outside on the porch in the swing. I wanted people to be able to hear us so that he didn't explode on me like I knew he was capable of. I told him I would not continue to live and be treated like that, and I didn't know what his problem was, but he better get rid of it if he wanted me around. I was mad; I was firm; I was blunt and straightforward. No ifs, ands, or buts… things had to be better, or we wouldn't be together. However, he said he truly didn't see anything he had done was so wrong even after I explained how I felt about all of it!

A few days after surgery, my daughter was allowed to come home but wasn't allowed to go back to school for two weeks. She required a tutor for the two weeks to come to the house so she could stay caught up on her schoolwork. I also had to become her nurse as the surgery had resulted in an open wound, which required new packings and dressings daily. During this time, my daughter, my husband, and I went to Chinese one evening for dinner, and my fortune cookie said, "Keep your plans secret for now," smiley faces too.

Well, I didn't think it was coincidence that my fortune cookie said what I was already feeling in my heart. Although we had gone to eat together, he was still being and acting like who he had shown he was on the inside… just not to that degree. `

It didn't take long, though, before he showed that same behavior. It was about a month after my daughter was able to go back to school, and I had gone home and had lunch with him, as I did most days since my work was about two minutes away. We had a quick lunch with nothing wrong, and I went back to work. About thirty minutes later, he came to my work and walked up to the window that was in front of me in the nursing home I worked in and took his pointer finger, and motioned for me to come to him… he had a frown on his face. I turned to my coworker, who was a very dear friend whom I had shared his behaviors with and my plans with, and I told her I didn't know what was about to happen, but I thought the s*** was about to hit the fan! She had seen him, and she said, "I think so too."

So, I walked out into the nursing home lobby and sat down with him, and he proceeded to tell me that after I left, he decided to have a talk with my son, who was seventeen at the time.

He tells me that he told my son that he wanted him to get a job. He continues and tells me that my son said, "I have a job, and you know I do because I am bringing the debris and dumping it on your land." He was tearing up a patio for someone to rebuild it but wasn't working on it that day because of the rain. So, my husband proceeded to tell me that he told my son, "I want you to get a real job so you can make real money, so you can give your mama money so she can give me money." He then says, "You know what your son said to me? He said that you were my responsibility." He then had the nerve to say to me, "It was all I could do to keep from beating the s*** out of him."

I wanted to shout, "Go, son!" I wanted to beat some sense into this man sitting in front of me. My heart ached; I hated that he felt he was in the right to impose this on my son and apparently thought I was going to be upset with my son… instead of with him!

I looked at him, in shock, I'm sure, and just shook my head and said, "Okay."

Strange, but if anything other than that took place, I don't recall it. But I vividly remember walking toward the door with him and watching him walk out the door of my workplace, and I knew the time was now; I knew that the Lord was letting me know the time was now, just as I had asked of Him, to let me know when!

I went to my desk and sat for a second and then went to the prayer closet (bathroom) and cried and prayed. I knew I had to set a plan in motion, and it had to be done now. So I went back to my office that I shared with my friend and told her what had transpired and told her I had to find a place… she agreed. I told her I had to talk to the administrator because I needed to leave… she agreed. So, I asked my administrator if I could talk to her as I was closing her door. I shared what had just happened with her, and she gave me her blessing to not only leave to find a place but told me the deposit would be covered. I couldn't have been more blessed at the time to work with all the wonderful, loving, caring, compassionate, Christian women that I did.

So, I left but knew that I had two important agendas. One, to find a place to go, and two, to let my kids know what was happening. Ironically, my oldest daughter and son were together. My daughter had moved back from college and was renting a house from my husband, and my son was at her house washing my dear work friend's car in the back. It was such a heavy burden to have to share what had happened with them. Not just what had happened today but what had been happening all along and especially when my youngest was in the hospital. I had been keeping all this from them.

He was even bitter when my son would come in at night and come down the hall to our *open* bedroom door and say, "Mom, I'm home. I love you," before going upstairs to bed.

He would sometimes angrily ask me, "Why does he have to do that?"

My only response was, "Because he does love me." I couldn't understand why that was an issue for him when his son would *come in* and go through our bedroom to the bathroom and shower and come back out at all times of the night, and I never complained, even at four in the morning, but neither did he.

So many of his thought processes I couldn't comprehend.

Like the time when it was rumored at church that two church members that were married were having an affair. The lady had a beautiful voice and was always singing songs, but due to the rumor, or the truth, she had stepped down from singing and had been absent from church for a while, and the gentlemen she was accused of having the affair with was continuing to attend with his wife and children. The lady came to church one morning and was sitting right in front of us, and my husband sat there, in church, and blatantly shook his head. I asked what he was shaking his head about, and he advised me that he didn't need to come to church with people like that. I got so upset with him that it was hard for me to focus on the sermon. I couldn't believe that he was judging her so harshly over something that, first, he had no way of knowing was true, and second, what better place for her to be, whether it was true or not. When we got home, I questioned him about it. He said, "I don't need to go to church with g** d*** people like that." I couldn't believe his perception of sin. So, I told him that what just came out of his mouth was as much a sin as what he was accusing or believing, because he didn't know if it was true, and even if it was, it isn't for us to judge. I told him that the Lord doesn't measure sin; people do, but sin is sin! Both adultery and taking the Lord's name in vain are one of the Ten Commandments, and they are not measured separately, but both are sinful, and what better place to come to for forgiveness or healing?

Maybe it wasn't his thought processes I couldn't comprehend, but more importantly, his heart processes instead! You can lead a horse to water, but you can't make him drink!

As I mentioned earlier, I had been in much prayer about the situation and had earnestly, prayerfully, and tearfully sought the Lord's will and His discernment as to when the time was appropriate for me to leave. I had been continuously praying and waiting on the Lord's timing, not mine. I was also putting complete faith in my discussion with the Lord that day in the park, and the fact that my fortune cookie, which I truly believed was a message from the Lord, read, "Keep your plans secret for now!" I had also taken it to work with me and taped it on my computer so I could see it!

Well, there was absolutely no doubt in my mind, my heart, my body, my spirit, and my soul that the Lord was speaking loudly and clearly that the time was now! So, I put a plan into action that very day!

After telling my oldest daughter and son what had been happening all this time, my son immediately told me he knew of a place that was available for us to rent. He said that some of his friends had just moved out, and he knew the man that owned it and told me to come, and he would take me there. We pulled up to this beautiful little house with a wraparound porch and went up the steps, and knocked on the door. The door was ajar and opened enough so that I could see in and saw a table and chairs inside. Since the door opened, my son said, "Come on in, and I will show you." Well, it was small but quaint inside, but I explained to my son that it wasn't big enough because it only had two bedrooms, and we needed three. He excitedly told me that we had to go outside and up the stairs into the attic portion, which was a complete room up there that encompassed the entire length of the downstairs that could be his bedroom. So, we went out and up. As I stood there gazing around, I saw a stack of mattresses in the corner. About six twin-sized mattresses. I said, to myself, *Those are my beds*. I had been sleeping on a $20,000 antique bed every night, but I was so excited to see that stack of twin-sized mattresses the Lord had piled in that corner for me!

So, as we went back down the stairs, the gentleman who owned the home had seen us there and came over. My son introduced us and advised this gentleman that we were needing a place, and he knew this was available because his friends had just moved out. Well, much to my dismay, the gentleman advised he had just rented it. I stomped my foot in disappointment, and he looked at me bewildered. I gave him my name and number and advised him if anything changed, to please give me a call. You see, I knew this was supposed to be my house because of the mattresses the Lord was providing, but he was telling me it wasn't going to be my house. Well, as we were departing, this gentleman stated, "Well, they didn't give me a deposit, and they do have a big dog and I don't want that, and she told me she had just been bitten by a brown recluse spider and the more I think about it if they move here, they may be bringing brown recluse spiders with them." I confidently advised him at this point to let me know if anything changed, and my son and I left.

The next morning as soon as I got to work, I received a call from him asking if I was still interested in his rental. I quickly expressed I was interested, and the next words out of his mouth were more confirmation that the Lord was not only giving me beds, but He was also in control of other financial concerns I had! I asked if those were his mattresses that were upstairs in that corner, and he said they were and I was welcome to use them. He also advised that electricity was already on and all I would have to do was pay the bill. Then he graciously advised that he also cuts the grass!

Wow! I got off the phone and was doing a circle dance while sharing with my dear coworker friend, as we worked in the same tiny office, and she began doing a circle dance with me. She also began asking me what I had to set up a home for myself again. I advised her I didn't know what I had and that I had some stuff in storage but had no idea what it was, but that I had given all my living room and dining room furniture to my daughter when she was in college. I specifically remember her asking if I had pictures. I also advised her I had given a lot of them to my daughter and sold some in a yard sale, and I honestly didn't have any idea what I did have.

So that night, I devised a plan to pack two weeks' worth of clothing and then the other necessary items for myself when he left the next morning to drive the school bus. You see, even though he was a millionaire, he drove a school bus for insurance. So, I grabbed everything I could for myself that morning, so it wouldn't be obvious to him when he returned. Later that afternoon, I went and picked up my youngest daughter from school prior to him picking her up on the bus, and we went home and did the same for her. I also had called my son and told him to do the same.

So, that night we didn't return to his house, but the three of us went to the house that the Lord provided for us!

Shortly after I arrived there, my dear friend also arrived and opened every car door and her trunk and began to shower me with everything we needed to not only exist in this house but to be completely sufficient with the costly living essentials of a home. Linens, including towels, washcloths, bedding, pillows, pillowcases, dinnerware, silverware, some pots and pans, paper towels, soap, shampoo, and on and on. One of the things I remember being the most overwhelming to me was a huge box of trash bags! You see, I hadn't ever been able to afford a box of trash bags that big, and especially not the expensive Glad bags they were. My dear friend, my precious more-than-seventy-year-old administrator, and her sister, who barely knew me, had all pitched in together and pulled things from their own homes to bless me with! My administrator had also graciously given me her cell phone to use as I didn't have one. As precious as that was, she was not that familiar with a cell phone either, and I realized it was dead, and I had no way to charge it. And don't forget, she also covered the deposit for the house!

So, I had asked my friend if she would be so kind as to come by and make sure I was up in time to get my daughter off to school. She said she would, but she didn't come by before I left to take her. Well, when I got to work, she came in shortly thereafter, apologizing for not coming to make sure I was awake as she promised. She also excitedly explained to me that she was coming, but she had seen two-yard sale signs on the way, and even though she had driven past them, when she got to the end of the road, something made her go back. She also explained there were two, one with a rich-looking sign and the other not so much, so she chose that one. She excitedly described to me that she had bought me some beautiful pictures. She explained they were huge and trimmed in gold and they were beautiful and that she couldn't wait to show them to me, so she was going to go back to her car and get them.

In the meantime, I went to the office across the hall to get myself a new badge made. She comes in and is standing in the hall with two pictures turned into her, so I can't see them. She turned one picture around and said, "Look, Trish, isn't this beautiful?" I was shocked, and I explained to her that it was my picture! Well, she is a blonde, and I say that lovingly, from her head to her toes. She said, "I know, Trish, I bought it for you."

I said, "No, Debbie, that is the picture I sold in a yard sale three years ago when I married George."

She said, "You are kidding," and I said, "No." She said, "Well, is this your picture too?" as she turned the other picture around.

I said, "That's my picture too," as I cryingly walked away and went to the far corner of the nursing home and squalled. It was unmistakably another confirmation from the Lord that He not only prepared a home for me to move into, but He was also giving me back some of the most prized pictures that I begrudgingly sold in the yard sale I had and gotten rid of these $10 pictures that I knew would not fit in his completely antique decorated home.

Well, when I regained composure of myself and went into our office, and we were still in awe of what had just transpired, it continued! She then picked up some bags and began pulling things out and asking if they were mine! She pulled out a sunflower clock, yes, mine. She pulled out some curtains, yes, mine! She pulled out a plaque of the Lord's prayer and asked if it was mine, and I told her no, but I was going to get on to Brandie for selling that. She advised that is who she wrote her check to. I began to ask her about another picture, and she said she was going to get it, but another woman walked up to get the two she had gotten at the same time as her, and that lady got the other one I was asking about. She said that Brandie had told her about some other things she bought at the same time as the pictures that she might want. I questioned her about some things, and she said she had seen some of those things. So, I called Brandie on the phone and told her I had left George and that I wanted all my stuff back.

She surprisingly asked me, "What?" I told her my friend had just come by and bought some of my stuff back for me, and I wanted everything she was selling back. She began saying, "Mama, give me that, and give me that," etc.… until finally, she said, "Okay, Trish, I have all your stuff." I told her to hang onto it and that I would get it from her.

Shortly thereafter, I received a call from Brandie, who explained she was on her way to work and asked me if I knew what this meant. I explained to her that I definitely knew what this meant. You see, I had ministered to Brandie, and she came and heard my testimony once and told me the next morning when she came in for work that she couldn't sleep that night and had gone home and shared it all with her husband, everything I had shared. She then advised me that she had cold chills all the way to work.

Well, the news of this had spread throughout the nursing home like wildfire. Everyone was coming into our office saying they had heard. Also, Brandie called me back and said she had gone to work and told everyone what had happened, and they all wanted to meet me and asked when I could come. I said, "Well, I go to lunch at 11:30." She didn't hesitate and yelled out to everyone that I was coming at 11:30! So, I advised Debbie that she was coming too because she was a big part of this wonderful story. Debbie and I went to this orthopedic office to share and rejoice over this wonderful thing that the Lord had done. As I walked in the door, Brandie said to me, "I told everyone they would know who you were when you come in because you glow." Wow, what an awesome perception of me from someone! I was very humbled but proud at the same time because I knew it wasn't my glow she was referring to but the Lord's glow in me! Well, it got more beautiful as her and all her coworkers came out into the patient waiting room, and we stood there amongst the patients and shared and praised the Lord for what had happened. And then, low and behold, Brandie looked at me and said, "You were always the example of what a Christian should be when I worked with you." She also said, "I've got every note you ever left me on my desk." I don't even remember doing it, and I told her so, but she said, "I would be having a rough time or a bad day, and I would leave my desk and come back, and you had left me a note." She then said one of the most powerful statements anyone has ever said to me that also made me understand what my dream, which I shared with you earlier, was about. She boldly stated, "I can tell y'all what the Lord wants Trish to do, and that is to bring people to Him!" And I say, "Here I am, Lord, use me!"

Wow! This statement made the whole puzzle, and the years of Wonderment make complete and total sense! The fact that she Just stood there in that office, in front of all those strangers, to me, and Declared that it was not only humbling but one of the biggest compliments (That just happened as I was writing this!—WWJD) and blessings I had ever received because it brought my dream to life!

Needless to say, I didn't get any work done that entire day. Every employee in that entire facility heard this beautiful story and came to share and express their happiness over this blessing. Later that day, as I was walking down the hall, the occupational therapist said as she was walking past me that it was going to be on the radio next week. I questioned what she was talking about, and she said she had a friend that worked at a Christian radio station in Macon, and she had called and shared this story, and they were going to put the story on the radio. Ironically it ended up on three stations after Debbie and I went to a church in town for a fundraiser and began to share. It was shared on that station in Griffin and then another one they told us about.

I had also told my administrator that day that I was sorry that I had not gotten any work done at all that day. She replied, "Well, did you leave anything important out?" I responded, "No, I don't guess I did!"

You see, it was an entire day of sharing, rejoicing, and praising the Lord for His miraculous, undeniable work amid unbearable pain, hardship, trials, tribulations, and pure heartache!

Praise the Lord!
Amen! Amen! And Amen!

P.S. I left without all the jewels he had adorned me with. My administrator told me those were presents and I should have taken them. I told her it was more important for me to leave them to show him money and jewels were not important and that if the Lord wanted me to have jewelry, He would give them to me! I was adorned with loads of jewelry from my coworkers! The only thing I really miss is all the beautiful cameo pieces I had.

CHAPTER 10
Confusion in the Midst

2006–2010: Ages Fifty-Two Through Fifty-Six

Well, it has been a couple of months now since I have sat down and shared. I gave myself six months to write this book after I began again on August 26, 2015, and I am a few days within my six months goal, which ironically will be my dad's eighty-sixth birthday.

I have, I must admit, gone through another time of depression or suppression, as all of the feelings I have shared and need to share in this chapter have brought back many unpleasant and unhappy memories. This chapter, however, was the most recent of the hard times that I have endured but was by no means the least stressful.

I had moved to a small town in East Georgia with my youngest daughter who was in the sixth grade. I moved onto sixteen acres of land that my father gave me and purchased a mobile home... on my own. My daughter and I settled in, although, in the beginning, she was very upset with me because she had to leave her friends and move to a town where she didn't know anyone. I began looking for work and soon found out that I may have made a big mistake because the only job I could find in town offered me $9, which was at the courthouse. I had to turn it down and told them I was a single parent with no child support and would not be able to keep what I just had gotten on $9 per hour. I was still very disappointed to find that a one-hour drive to the next major town only offered $11 per hour with a temp service. I had no choice but to accept. So, needless to say, it was a struggle and honestly still is even though I have found full-time employment and received three promotions and I have been well compensated above that now. It is, however, still a challenge to have a single income while trying to help my youngest daughter get a college degree by paying her car payment, car insurance, and health insurance while she covers the rest of her living expenses and takes out school loans. I am proud to say that all three of my children either have or have worked toward getting a college degree.

Well, when I moved to this small town, I had already begun to pray for what I envisioned to be the man of my dreams. I was still a hopeless believer in a wonderful, fulfilling partnership. However, I wasn't ready to just jump for any man that may come my way or be introduced to me.

I was approached by my neighbor, who was a deacon of the church I was attending, who suggested I go to dinner with his friend. His friend, however, was close to my father's age, so I politely refused. He told me that he was a wealthy man who just needed a friend and needed to give the old ladies of the church something to talk about. I was offended but politely told him that would not be me… that they were talking about, I mean. He went on to tell me that he had bought his previous girlfriend a $55K car, and then she left him. I don't know if that was supposed to entice me or what, but it didn't work. After what I had already been through with a wealthy man, I didn't care to go there again.

Then I was introduced to a local man whose wife had passed away. He had two sons, and he had invited me over for dinner one evening, and we had a pleasant time, and he seemed nice enough. We began to talk a lot on the phone, and I really liked the companionship. So, we had a couple more visits. He visited my house one weekend when I had my grandchildren. We met one evening and had pizza in town. Then he invited me to his house for dinner again, and this time it was just he and I. We ate and then began watching a movie. He asked if I wanted to see his house. He began showing me around and then bluntly asked if we were going to be together or not. I told him that

I liked him a lot, but I wasn't ready to be in a physical relationship. I explained to him that I had made that mistake with my previous relationship, and I felt that I moved too quickly and was, therefore, in a physical relationship before I was in an emotional one, and I didn't want to make that mistake again. As I left, we hugged, and I told him not to take what I had said personally and please try to understand that I wanted to wait until we grew more, emotionally, and I hugged him and patted him as I did so. He responded by saying to me, "You don't have to pat me on the back; I ain't no d*** baby." That was the last conversation we had. That was definitely not the kind of emotion I was looking for.

So, two and a half years had passed since I had moved while I was hoping for Mr. Right, and I was introduced to a friend of a coworker and her husband. They set up a blind date for us to go to have dinner at their house so we could meet. There was an immediate attraction, but I still had the walls built up that I wasn't planning to easily let down. But my walls tumbled when later that night, my coworker's husband told me that if anything happened to him that he wouldn't mind one bit if his wife ended up with this man. I had never heard such a compliment and knew that this man must be as awesome as I perceived him to be for him to say that about him. I let my guard completely down, and I fell hard and fast. I fell too hard and too fast and went headfirst into this relationship with blinders on. For a year, we were together every chance we got, and I took chances I shouldn't have. I still had my daughter, my son, and my oldest daughter and her husband had moved in with me at the time, so I took every opportunity I could to go see and be with him. All three of my children had tried to convince me that this man was different than what I perceived him to be. I was very upset and hurt with them and tried to convince them that he was the most wonderful thing that had ever happened to me, and he would be for them, too, if they just gave him a chance. They tried to make me see that there had to be a major problem with a man who had a daughter that he had not seen for five years. He made excuses, and my blinders wouldn't allow me to see what my children could see and feel.

I look back on it now and see how foolish and immature I was, even at my age, but for the first time in my life, I was head over heels in love and, yes, lust. So, about a year later, he asked me when we were going to get married. I was thrilled that he was the one looking at the calendar and trying to come up with a date instead of me. So, we had a beautiful simple wedding outside at some of his friend's house after he had surprised me with the money for it that he explained he got from his mom. One thing I didn't understand the night of our wedding was when I was dancing and talking to his younger brother; he looked at me very seriously and said, "You keep the checkbook." I was perplexed by that comment, and unfortunately, it didn't take long to find out exactly what he meant.

My new husband moved into my house because the little one-bedroom cabin that his mom had built him, uh oh, was too little for us, considering I had a daughter as well as the fact that she was in school in a completely different county. Before we married, my oldest daughter and her husband had moved out, so in the beginning it was he and I, my son, and my youngest daughter. Not long after we were married, my son left for California but not before my husband began to show how possessive he was of me. There were times when we would all be there, and he would go to the bedroom, and if I sat down in the living room to spend some time with my children, even for five minutes, instead of going to the bedroom with him, he would present himself with his arms thrown up in the air and question me if I was coming. It was awkward that he would do that in front of my children, so I would tell him that I would be there in a minute. If I didn't go when he thought I should, I guess, he would come back a little while later and throw his arms up in the air again, eyebrows raised, and angrily say, "You coming?" It became apparent to me very quickly that I was in a tough situation. I had tried to convince my children that he would be wonderful for them if they gave him a chance, but it was quickly apparent to me, as well as my children, that he didn't want a chance. I tried to explain to him the situation that put me in with my children and how it looked to them, but he could care less and continued to do it and blamed it on what they were watching. Even when I asked him to come and sit down with us, and we could watch a movie or something, it didn't matter to him; he would go to the bedroom and be mad at me if I didn't follow him. Nothing I did or said made him see the harm he was causing not only with our relationship but also with the unformed relationship he didn't and wouldn't have with my children if he continued that behavior.

I began to feel trapped and felt like a prisoner in my own home. I know my children felt that way too, but even worse for them because their mom was being held prisoner, away from them, in their own home. My daughter questioned me as to why I had to be locked up in the bedroom all the time. Of course, there was no answer for that, and all I could do was tell her that I questioned that myself but to no avail. Because every time we went in the bedroom, he would close and lock the door, even if I asked him not to, even if we were just watching TV, and he made it apparent to me that he was closing and locking it, no matter what. I have always been very close to my children, and I felt he wanted me to choose between them and him. Instead of being a part of us, I felt he wanted to tear my children and me apart.

Sadly, they felt that too.

I was still trying hard and was still committed to making this relationship work, and I wanted and tried to work through the hurdles. Even the hurdles I had to jump after he quit job after job, after job, after job, after job, after job. Yes, within a year and eight months after our marriage had begun, he had quit his sixth job and was adamantly telling me he was going to quit the seventh. Well, you can imagine the hardship and strain that was putting on our relationship too.

I was only making $13.50 dollars an hour at a new job. I had worked for 364 days at the previous job that I hated going to every day. I worked in a nursing home, and the administrator was the meanest person I had ever met in the workplace. She was very rude to almost all her employees and picked a select few to bully and be particularly mean to, and I was lucky enough to be selected as one of those. I have never met or worked with anyone like her, but I stuck it out, like I said, for 364 days, because I had to have an income. I couldn't just get mad and leave; I just had to turn the other cheek, unlike my husband, although his advice was to just quit. He didn't pay any of the bills when he did work but expected me to pay what bills he had when he quit job after job, etc. Lots of times, even when he had a job, he had no money and was always holding out his hand to me. It was very hard on me, but I was willing to stand by him and work through his tough times. It became apparent, though, when I found a job to replace the one I had for 364 days, and I hated every minute of it, but was going to have to take a $2.50 cut to take it, my husband, who so readily quit jobs and thought it was okay, strongly insisted that I not take that job because of a pay cut. He insisted that I call his stepfather, who, he insisted, would set me straight.

I called his stepfather and explained the situation I was in and the future I could see with the new position, which would also allow me to have insurance on my husband, which he didn't have. Fortunately, his stepfather advised me to accept the position and deal with my husband later. He also advised me that they have always had to financially support my husband at times, and this is not the first and wouldn't be the last time that they have had to go against his thoughts on financial issues. He was already asking them for money all the time since he was quitting his jobs because I just didn't have it to give him anymore. He had graciously helped me go through a very large sum of back child support I had gotten. His mom had called me at one point and said he was asking for money, and they didn't want to give it to him anymore, but she wanted me to let her know if we needed it, and she would give it to me. I wasn't comfortable asking them for money and told her that. I also shared with her that I had never had to borrow money from my parents except once in my life, and it was the hardest thing for me to have to do. She called me a few days later to come by their house to pick up a check that she had made out to me. She told me my husband had asked for $650, and she wanted to give it to me. She and her husband also told me that the happiest time in their lives was when they didn't see my husband for five years because he always asked for and needed money. They explained he had always had a never-ending need for money. She said five years had passed, and they had not seen or heard from him, and she heard the doorbell ring and looked and saw his eyes and knew he was there for money. She said he left that day with five thousand dollars! Wow!

Although all this information was alarming and disappointing news, it shed a whole new light on my situation, and I felt maybe I finally understood his brother's comment, on our wedding day, about the checkbook, or at least I thought I did. But now I had to figure out what to do with the information I was given because it was definitely something that I couldn't discuss with my husband, considering the source and the relationship involved. So, I kept this information to myself, but it made me a little wiser and a lot more cautious.

You see, up until this point, I had been very trusting and had even given him my debit card several times for gas to look for a job, and I didn't keep check on what he was doing with it. Needless to say, I was shocked when I checked my account and found that in three days' time, he had taken $200 out, and I didn't have any idea. I knew there was no way his little Toyota truck could have used that much gas. When I asked him why he had taken that much money, which was cash withdrawals, out of my account in three days' time and what he had done with it, he had no answer except that it was a few weeks earlier and he didn't know. I told him I couldn't afford those kinds of withdrawals, considering I was only making between $11 or $13 per hour at the time and considering all the obligations I had that I wouldn't be able to pay even my bills and certainly not his bills too.

So, needless to say, I wasn't so trusting with my debit card anymore.

However, this new information shed a whole new light on a lot of things that I had been noticing, not understanding, and not confronting. Even when he did work, he never had money and was always asking me to front him some. Of course, it was always that he would give it back, but I never got it back. He never helped with any of the household bills either, although I didn't ask. I guess I was used to not having anyone to lean on and I didn't lean on my new husband. On the other hand, he didn't step up to the plate and offer either, but he sure didn't have a problem leaning on me.

I felt I had to reassess our entire relationship. I decided to make a few phone calls to get input from his brother and sister because now I had a lot of unanswered questions. His brother informed me that he had recently borrowed a substantial amount from him as well, which I knew about, but I explained to him that I had no idea why he needed it or what he had done with the money. We agreed that he wouldn't give him any more money, and he also agreed that my husband needed to get and keep a job.

His sister informed me that their father died owing a lot of money on his home place because he kept borrowing against it to give my husband money. She said she had told her father many times not to borrow or give him any more money, but he would always do it anyway.

His brother and sister both informed me that he had a very bad gambling habit and would spend a lot of time and a lot of money playing the lottery. I never will forget the devastation I felt when his sister told me, "He will leave you penniless." Her next statement about him was that he was a narcissist. I even had to ask her what that meant because, although I knew the word, I didn't know the meaning. When I heard the meaning, I knew I not only knew the word now but was living with its meaning! This one word helped me understand his unrelenting prodding and badgering about my two previous husbands as well.

Needless to say, these two conversations were just as alarming and devastating as the information I was previously given by his parents. I was shocked with myself that I could be so blinded, trusting, and gullible after all I had already been through. But they say love is blind, and I was definitely in love with what and whom I thought I knew or wanted so desperately to believe I had found.

So, the walls are closing in on me, but I have to hold them at bay!

Again, I was in a predicament where I had been given loads of very important information that I could do or say nothing about because of the sources and relationships involved. Needless to say, all this news was both heartbreaking and mind-boggling. Then, I had to figure out what to do with this valuable information.

I decided the only way we were going to make it through this was if I was smart about my decisions and actions. I secretly—and he still doesn't know it to this day—began going to his vehicle in the middle of the night to find his lottery tickets to see what and how much money he was spending on this habit, considering he didn't have a job. For a week, I snuck out of the house in the middle of the night and found each day that he had spent $15 a day on mega tickets. It's possible that he bought scratch-offs, but there was no need to keep those, so I never found any. But for someone who was making what I was and considering he wasn't working, that was way too much to be spending a day on them. Fifteen dollars a day times thirty days added up to be my house payment for a month, which I wouldn't have my house payment if it was my $15 a day he was spending. But he was surely about to exhaust all his other money avenues, so whose $15 a day would it be then?

I decided after my investigation and discussing it with his brother, who said my husband would be furious, that I had to just talk to him. I told him that I wanted him to quit playing the lottery because I knew it was something he was spending money we didn't have, especially since he wasn't working. I used the example that if you spend, say, $15 a day on the lottery, then in thirty days, you have spent $450, which adds up to be a lot of money. Surprisingly, he said okay and didn't get mad and said he knew that was coming. I was relieved. I trusted him, but it wasn't long before I saw a new ticket in his truck one day when we were going somewhere though so he really didn't quit like he said he would.

I also explained to him that he had to keep this job that he was threatening to quit, especially until he found another one because I couldn't continue to keep both of our bills paid, and it wasn't fair to his parents for him to be asking them for money. He said his mom had been trying to convince him of that exact thing, but he said he couldn't make any promises and spout out a few profanities about the job and the people that he worked with. He had a very hot temper and had even threatened some of his previous employers that he would beat them up and if he got put in jail that his mom, uh oh, would get him out, and he would come and beat them up again. I was in shock when he proudly told me that was what he had told his bosses at the job he quit a few months after we were married. I couldn't believe that my mid-fifties husband was proudly proclaiming that he would beat his bosses up a second time after his mom, uh oh, got him out of jail. The fact that he would brag to me about that behavior showed me a lot about him that I didn't know!

Nevertheless, I still tried to maintain my composure and work with him through these difficulties. I have just had an epiphany that he didn't even realize, at that time or even now, how difficult of a situation I knew I was in since the newfound knowledge I was given from his family.

It continued to be a constant struggle for his mom and me to try to make him understand the importance of him keeping his job until he could find a replacement. The more he threatened to quit, the harder we tried to convince him why he shouldn't and couldn't. It didn't matter to him, though; he was determined he was quitting. It all made sense now to me that when we were dating, and his father was still living, every time he called my husband, I heard him tell him he needed to keep his job. I didn't know there was a history of jumping from job to job.

His mom and I were on the phone one day discussing his unwillingness to accept the fact that he needed to keep his job, and I told her that if he did quit that I was going to have to ask him to leave because I couldn't afford to lose my home by continuing to help him. She said she understood but asked me not to send him her way if I asked him to leave. I told her it was her responsibility to keep her door locked if he came knocking on her door for money. Especially since he was a grown man and capable of making money to sustain himself, he just wasn't willing. Since she had already built him a home, he only had a truck payment, cable bill, and phone bill, which were all in his mom's name, uh oh, and an electric bill. But he would have to begin paying his truck insurance, too, since that was on the same policy with all my vehicles, and I was already paying it. Altogether his bills were approximately $600 per month, if that much, and for the life of me, I couldn't understand why he was unwilling to keep a job until he could find another so he could pay his obligations instead of expecting his mom or me to pay it and I didn't have it to pay for him anymore.

I will never forget him getting so mad at me one day when he asked me for money to pay his truck payment, and I told him I didn't have the money. He began pacing the floor and demanding to know what I had done with my tax money. I had gone to a festival with my sister, and she kept telling me to buy myself stuff, and I told her I couldn't, that I didn't need to spend the money. She kept insisting that I buy myself something. I would tell her that I couldn't, and she would say, "But you need that, and it would look so good on you," and I would tell her no, and she would say again, "But you need that," and I finally realized she was right. It was my money, and it wasn't right that I was keeping it to give to him in case he did quit. It wasn't so much that I really needed what she was insisting I needed, but more importantly, that I needed to realize that I was being an enabler. So, I spent my money on something for me. He was still working, and there was no rational reason for him not to have the money for his truck payment, but he didn't. He was furious when I told him I really didn't know how I had spent it but also told him that he should have the money. He was furious because he knew he was going to have to ask his mom, especially since the truck was in her name, and he couldn't be late with the payment. So, he had caused the problem by doing who knows what with his money but got mad at me because I couldn't bail him out because I had spent my money.

A few days later, his parents asked me to come by their house after work. His mom told me that he told her that he was having to spend so much money on gas was why he didn't have the money for his truck payment. I told her that is what he told me, but I knew it wasn't true because I traveled way further than he did, and his little truck got a lot more gas mileage than mine did, and I didn't spend that much money on gas. She pulled out a piece of paper where they had done the mileage and gas calculations. I told her I had already done the calculations in my head, and what he was saying didn't add up. She told me not to let him see that piece of paper, or he would know it was her writing.

So there I was again, being told and shown by his parents that neither they nor I should trust my husband, and neither they nor I truly knew what he was doing with money.

So, needless to say, we were all at a breaking point!

In addition to all this, there was more upsetting to me; he had recently done and said some inappropriate things in the presence of my young daughter.

But here I was a year and eight months later in something that I wasn't even sure what it was that I was in. One thing I did know, though, was that I was in something not necessarily way over my head but way over my ability to solve. I learned long ago that there are some things you can't fix, and sometimes you must give up trying. If there is one thing in my relationships that I have had to try desperately to hold onto, it is my own sanity. I could see that this was a situation that I could end up losing everything. I could lose my children, my home, and possibly my sanity, and after what I had been through, I decided it wasn't worth it.

So, after much prayer and lots of discussions with my sister, because I really had to talk to someone about all this, I decided I had to ask him to leave. I never wanted to end another marriage. But I also knew this man had already done a lot of damage to the ones that were nearest and dearest to me, and I couldn't stand by and let him destroy my entire family. I remember when we first met how excited I got when he told me he used to be in a gospel band. I just knew that I had met the man that was going to love me like Christ loves the church. Well, unfortunately, my vision was wrong, but I got confirmation that I was doing the right thing when I asked him to leave.

On Friday night, March 8, 2010, he was adamantly pronouncing that he was going to quit his job again. I told him again that he couldn't quit until he found another one because I couldn't pay both of our bills. He took his fist and slammed it down on the kitchen counter and said, "I am quitting this job, and I don't care if it makes m***** f****** Jesus Christ mad, do you hear me?"

Well, that was Friday night. I don't really recall much that happened from Friday to Sunday because I was in turmoil, but on Sunday, I asked him to leave. As you can imagine, it didn't go over very well with him. He accused me of not standing by him, and I thought at one point he was going to hit me. I stood my ground and firmly told him to just leave as he was following me to our bedroom and trying to come in as I was closing the door behind me.

Like I said earlier, he still didn't know all that I knew and the many reasons I had to not stand by him, but more importantly, *I had to stand for myself* as well as my young daughter who was still living with us also.

I can't tolerate anyone, much less my husband, so disrespectfully using that kind of profanity in my home.

I More Than Survived the Storms

2010–2016

Today is Sunday, December 6, 2015, and although I haven't finished chapters nine and ten, I feel led to work on my final chapter, "I More Than Survived the Storms."

I just watched the movie *The Big Fish*. I turned it on last night and fell asleep very shortly into the movie. I woke up during his visit to Septor and again during his lake dive to catch the snake that was about to reach the naked lady in the lake. So, I woke up the next morning and thought, *I won't even waste my time watching this movie… because it is not worth watching*. Well, thankfully, I decided to watch it. You might ask, "Why?"

Well, I cried like a baby after it was over and realized that some of you who read my book might not believe some of the stories or experiences I have shared. They are all true, however, just as *The Big Fish's* son found his father's horrendous, unbelievable stories to be.

They are about my life and the experiences I have had. I feel it is important to share them with the world for two reasons!

The **first reason** is so you can see that while we may go through many trials and tribulations in life, what matters is what we do with those trials and tribulations that are the most important. I once saw a quote that states,

"Don't let other people or things upset you. They are powerless; your reaction is their only power!"

If we all learned those key things early in life, then life would be better for us all!

I took this quote and cut it out and taped it on my kitchen window, where I would see it every time I stand there and wash dishes! I was going through a tough time and another trial with my last husband when I found it... it helped! It is still there today, and I hope it will remain long after I am gone!

You see, although I have been through many hardships, hurt, and pain, I have nothing but joy in my life, which may be hard for some people to understand.

Although I live in a used mobile home that I bought for $18K, I am blessed!

Although I have very few nice things, since most of my belongings were either given to me, or purchased at yard sales, or out of dumpsters, or on the side of the road, I am blessed!

Although I drive a 2004 Town and Country Chrysler with 164K miles on it, and I am still paying for it, I am blessed!

Although I live from paycheck to paycheck, And have been overdrawn at times, I am blessed!

Although my three children have witnessed and endured the hardships with me, they are my friends as well as my children, I am blessed!

Although I am alone, as I am not married and live alone, I am not alone, I am blessed!

Although I have faltered and continue to do so, I still have the "Father" who I turn to for my source of comfort, And He comforts me! I am blessed!

As I sit here typing this, I can't help but have tears of both sorrow and joy. Although I have experienced the hurt and pain, I have, I can honestly say I wouldn't change anything if I could.

You see, what I have gone through has brought me to the place I am today.

I have forgiven myself and those who have hurt me, and I love myself and those who have hurt me. Although I choose not to live with those who hurt me, it doesn't mean that I can't love and forgive them in Christ! Just as Jesus said on the cross, forgive them, for they know not what they do.

I have come to realize that not all of us understand life in the same way or kindness, love, or forgiveness in the same way.

My first chapter was about my childhood and the unkindness of my father. Currently, my father is in a nursing home. I have been concerned about his salvation but have found it harder to discuss Jesus with him than I did the strangers in prison. I don't think my fear was actually talking to him about Jesus, but the possibility of his rejection of the talk.

You see, my father was deathly sick a few years ago, probably in late 2010, and had previously asked me to speak at his funeral after I had the honor of speaking at my sister's funeral in March 2010. His words were, "I didn't know you could preach… will you preach at my funeral?" Although I was honored, and I told him I would, immediately, I knew that I must know where his heart was in order to preach, as he put it, at his funeral.

When my father was deathly sick in the hospital, my neighbor's wife was my father's nurse. I had visited with my neighbor, who was a deacon of the church and a friend of my father's, and he asked me if my father was saved. I told him that I didn't know, and it was hard for me to talk to him about it. He said, "Well, let's go talk to him together." As we entered his ICU room, he began to tear up and told us that he was dying. My neighbor told him that we needed to talk to him about something then. He said, "We need to know if you are saved." My father responded, "I'm a good ol' boy." My neighbor and I both tried to explain that just being a "good ol' boy" wasn't what we needed to know. We asked him again and tried to explain about salvation, but all we could get out of him was that he was a "good ol' boy." So, we left frustrated that we couldn't make him understand but also knew that it wasn't words we could put into his mouth or his heart.

This weighed on me from 2010 to 2014. I went and picked my dad up from the nursing home one day to bring him home for a few hours. He started singing, "Jesus, you are my only friend," as he had done a few times before while sitting on the porch while visiting at home. This time, since we were alone, I took this as an opportunity to discuss his salvation with him, again. I asked where he had learned that song. He said he didn't know. I asked if he remembered asking me to preach at his funeral when my sister died. He said he did. I asked him if he still wanted me to. He said he did. I asked him what he wanted me to tell people. He said, "You can tell them anything you want." I asked, "Do you want me to tell them you're a good ol' boy?" He said, "Yeah." I reminded him of mine and the neighbor's visit a few years back and our conversation. I said, "Well, in order to speak at your funeral, I need to know if you are saved." He questioned, "Saved?" I said, "That simply means, do you believe in Jesus?" He said, "Yeah!" I said, "Do you want to live for Him, and do you want Him in your heart?" He said, "Yeah!" I said, "Well, you are saved then. So, if anyone asks you if you are saved again, the answer is 'yes.' That is all it means, that you believe in Jesus and want Jesus in your heart and to live for Jesus." He said, "Okay."

> *So, I now can rest in Jesus until that time comes that I can preach at his funeral and know that he is saved.*
> *I can and have forgiven him for all the hurt that not only I went through as a child but also my siblings… and especially my sister!*

Although my sister is no longer living, as I said, I can forgive him for her. You see, she and I had a conversation once that brought an enlightened sense of the deep pain and hurt she had experienced as a child. She said that she would not attend our father's funeral. I was perplexed by this statement, and she said that a funeral is to show your respects to that person, and she didn't respect him. I tried to convince her that she should go, and she said she would not. However, I totally understood why she felt the way she did.

Well, she didn't have the opportunity as she passed before him. As I mentioned before, I had the honor of speaking at her funeral. I don't recall when the previous conversation had transpired, but I'm sure it was before the story I'm about to share, because the day my sister passed, she had not only insisted but also taken our father to the doctor. He had been sick, and she insisted he go and see a doctor. It wasn't long before he ended up in the hospital deathly sick, but he made it through it in the previous story I shared.

My sister had always lived away, as her husband was a thirty-year Navy officer, which caused them to live in many different and far away states, but we were always close. Her husband had retired, and they built a home and moved to the small town I lived in and across the field from my father, me, and my youngest brother. We all had our own places, but we all lived together on the family land. My sister and I had become even closer, since we lived closer, and we talked a lot. I had gone to her house one day to use her computer to work on my resume as I had been out of work for about a month and needed to update it. She was sitting on the bed in her bedroom where the computer was, and as I was typing, she said she needed to talk to me. I stopped and turned to her and said, "Okay." She tearfully reached into her pocket and explained to me that she had a suicide note in her pocket. I was shocked and dismayed because, from my standpoint, my sister had everything in life one would or should need to make them happy. She had a wonderful husband that loved her, a beautiful home and furnishings galore, a nice car, and two grown boys. I questioned her reasoning, and she explained she wanted to do it for her husband. She explained that she could see the toll it was taking on him having to work in that hot building he was working in. You see, he had taken a job to substantiate their income because although they had built a home here, they still owned another in our childhood hometown that their two boys were renting, and both had lost their jobs and weren't able to pay the rent on that place. This was when the economy had dropped, and homes weren't selling or weren't worth what they previously were, and lots of people were losing their jobs. I had actually walked out on mine. Something I didn't think I would ever do and was completely against my morals, but I was in a situation where I was working for a contracted agency, and an employee of the company I was contracted to work for reported my director for being abusive to us three women that worked for him and the company I was contracted with tried to blame me and use me as a scapegoat. That is why I was there using her computer.

But... back to my sister. So, as I said, I was shocked and hurting for her that she would be contemplating suicide. So, I began to question why. She said if she did, then her husband would get the money he needed to live a better life and not have to work. She said they had a lot of debt and taxes, and she didn't know how they were going to pay them. I asked her if she had discussed this with her husband and if she knew where they were financially. She said she hadn't talked to him about it and that he handled all the finances, but she had sat there on the computer the night before and cried. I told her she needed to discuss their finances with him. That everything was probably okay, but even if they weren't, her husband or her kids wouldn't want her to do this and would rather have her than money. I explained the guilt they would feel. Her husband wouldn't be happy if she wasn't there with him and if her sons knew that, they would have guilt because they weren't able to pay.

But the most important thing I realized at this time was her salvation. I asked her whether she knew if she would go to heaven if she died. She said she didn't and explained to me that she could never go up in front of the church and accept the Lord because of what Betty Sue had said to me. You see, I mentioned that when I went up and accepted Christ one week after my mom passed that my entire family was there. Well, my childhood neighbor was also present, as it was her church and her pastor that spoke at my mom's funeral. Well, about two weeks after accepting Christ, my neighbor, Betty Sue, called me at my home. She explained to me that she was calling because she knew that I wasn't raised in church, and she needed to let me know that I didn't do it right. I questioned what she meant, and she told me that when I went up that I was supposed to then turn around and tell the entire church that the Lord had just saved me. I explained to Betty Sue that I was actually saved from five to seven in the morning on Thursday while I was on the phone with her pastor because I couldn't take it anymore. I asked her how she was saved. She said she was saved in her home watching Billy Graham. I questioned who she then turned to and said the Lord had just saved her. She said she didn't have to and that it was different. I politely excused myself and told her it was nice talking to her, but I knew I was saved. As we hung up, I just shook my head at her perception of my salvation.

So that being said, I had shared this with my sister. She and her husband had continued to visit that church for a while, but she explained to me she couldn't make herself do it for fear she would do it wrong. I told her that we had talked about Betty Sue and her perception and that she was wrong. You don't have to tell anyone; it is between you and the Lord.

So, I told her that before I left, under the circumstances, she was going to know if she was saved or not. I asked, "Do you believe in the Lord?" She said, "Yes." I said, "Well, you are saved then. It doesn't have to be in a church or at an altar. If you believe and confess as you have done to me, then you are saved. It is as simple as that."

I went on to express to her to pray to the Lord about her thoughts. I advised, "If you don't feel you know how to pray, simply write a letter to Him. Write a letter to Him and share all your worries and pain. Instead of a suicide note, write a note to Him." I told her that it broke my heart to hear that she was going through these thoughts. I told her to put herself in my shoes. I had been out of work for a month and had no money, and I was the only source of income for my fifteen-year-old daughter and me. I had moved here and got a mobile home and got a loan against my land that Dad had given both of us, sixteen acres each, and was in jeopardy of losing it all, but I wasn't worried; instead, I was trusting in the Lord to give me a job. I was trusting in the Lord to give me a job with enough pay to keep what I had.

Although it was difficult to find a job in this area paying more than $9 an hour, which I had to turn down because it wouldn't be enough, I was still trusting in Him for the right job with the right pay. I had to leave, but I left with a heavy heart, not knowing if she would be okay. I told her she could always call and talk to me if she needed to, no matter what time of day or night it was. I also suggested she begin watching Joyce Meyer, which I explained I watched every morning.

We never discussed this incident again, but she and I did go see Joyce Meyer together!

So, it was this incident that caused me the honor of speaking at her funeral. As I said, she and I never discussed this, nor did I share it with her husband until her passing. I came home that day and shared this with my kids, as I needed someone to talk to about it because I was so upset about it but knew it wasn't my place to tell anyone else.

So, I shared what had happened that day a few years back with her husband, the morning after she passed, and told him I would be honored to speak and could because I knew where she was. I let him decide if I shared the entire story or if I shared just that I knew she was saved. He later decided he wanted me to share just that she was saved.

I feel it is important to share with you because it also shows the turmoil we can go through within our own selves, as I previously shared about myself, which can cause us to think that we would be better off, and so would others, if we weren't here.

That is not true, but it is a lie from Satan, and it is unfortunate that so many fall victim to it!

For those of you who can't imagine ever contemplating taking your own life, then you have truly been blessed. It doesn't mean that we are crazy… it just means there is a lot of hurt and emotions that are in need of a savior! Thank God that we both found Him!

As for my marriages… I have no animosity toward any of my husbands. I have sorrow and hurt and pain, but most importantly, forgiveness!

Although I was married to my first husband for twenty-three years, it was twenty-three years of confusion that was brought to understanding by my salvation in the Lord. I could have stayed in that marriage, but I wouldn't be the Christian that I am today if I had. I would be a beaten down submissive wife whose God was her husband... by his teaching!

I would rather serve the Lord than any man!

My second marriage to a multimillionaire was three years of being reminded daily that I was poor. Although he was attracted to what he saw in me, which was Jesus, I realized I couldn't make him or give him the same. When a man with millions will not happily own a four hundred popup with you to share with your kids, there is a serious heart problem as well as a serious money problem.

I would rather be poor alone than being reminded of my poorness by my husband and his earthly riches!

My third marriage, to what I thought was the man of my dreams, turned out to be a marriage of a hidden past, his not mine, as I shared my entire past with him in writing shortly after we met, because I wanted him to know me and love everything about me!

He, however, kept his past, which was also a part of his present, to himself yet continuously reminded me of mine. It wasn't until I asked him to leave my house that his past began to come out of the woodwork from everyone who knew him, including his family. They explained to me that they thought I was the woman who was going to fix him. I told them that I was good, but I wasn't that good! And more importantly, I'm not God!

I would rather be a poor fool for the Lord than be a fool for someone who thinks his gender makes him a man!

As the title of this chapter states, "I Have More than Survived the Storms," **and I have!**

I have loved and I have lost along the way, but I found and haven't lost **my faith or my salvation!**

I have made mistakes along the way, but I found and haven't lost **my faith or my salvation!**

I have sinned along the way, but I found and haven't lost **my faith or my salvation!**

I haven't been perfect along the way, but I found and haven't lost **my faith or my salvation!**

I have made wrong decisions along the way and still do, but I found and haven't lost **my faith or my salvation!**

I have suffered along the way, **But I have found and kept my faith and my salvation!**

My Dash
1956–Beyond

As I relived the hurt and pain of my youth,
I took a year-long break before I could share more truth,
Truth about all the lessons that lay ahead,
I couldn't have dreamed them up as I lay in my bed!

Never would I have dreamt in a million years,
What the future held for me or the many tears,
Tears that would be shed over things that I did,
But He knew them all because from Him they are not hid!

Never would I have dreamt of what I would go through,
I would have chosen differently if I only knew,
What lay ahead for me and what was in my path,
If I could have avoided all the confusion and wrath!

But the walk I have taken has not been alone,
During this time, I have spent at my earthly home!
For the trials and tribulations that I have had,
Although they may have been hard and, at times, caused me to
*   be sad!*

Without them, I may not have searched for the Lord,
And found the love that I needed and adored!
Or the prayers that I prayed for many years,
As I went through these trials and shed many tears!

As I sang to the Lord many times in the shower alone,
While I'm sure, He sat and listened on His heavenly throne!

I sang, and I prayed!
for the Lord,
to prepare me,
to be a sanctuary,
to be pure and holy,
To be tried and true,
And with thanksgiving,
I'll be a living,
Sanctuary for You!

So, this testimony that you have just read,
Isn't any longer something that I dread,
To share with you so that you can also see,
All the wonderful things the Lord can do for both you and for
*   me!*

Although I have faltered many times, and the road has been
*   tough,*
Because Satan has tempted and taunted me and tried to call
*   my bluff,*
I know that I have won this battle on earth,

Because of the Lord and my rebirth!

Even though my hands may now be withered by time,
Only the Lord really knows what goes on in my heart and my
* mind!*
All the lines that may now be etched on my face,
I have earned them, each one, and wear them with grace!

These things that I have shared are not for my glory or fame,
But these things I have shared are to glorify His Holy name!
Amen!

Written on October 10, 2015, at 9:00 a.m.
Thank You, Jesus, for the roads I have traveled!
Amen!

CHAPTER 12

Life and Death

On February 22, I thought I had finished this book. February 22 was four days before the six-month deadline I had given myself to finish. What I am about to share with you, although it was difficult, I believe it was the Lord's plan for this to be the last chapter of my book... because I couldn't have planned this.

I went into work on February 23 and saw one of the prayer warriors that I mentioned in my dedication section. She was the one I mentioned who was giving me the extra special encouragement. I was walking into my office, and she was there speaking to another coworker, and she saw me, and I excitedly shared with her that I had finished my book. She was coming into my office to share her excitement with me, as well, and my phone rang. I told her it was the nursing home and it had to be about my dad. She said, "Okay, then, I will talk to you later," but also said how excited she was for me that I had finished and that she couldn't wait to read it.

I answered the phone to find that the voice on the other end of the line was calling to discuss a DNR (Do Not Resuscitate) form with me. They explained that although I had signed one when he was admitted, since that time, he had told them, at some point, that he wanted them to save him. They also advised that they didn't think he understood what that really meant. I told them that I was sure he didn't understand the ramifications and that neither he nor his kids would want him to go through that. Especially considering he would be eighty-six in three days, and that would just be prolonging the inevitable. They explained that since I had the POA, I could sign another one on his behalf since neither of us thought he really understood what he was requesting they do.

While I agreed to sign another one, I also questioned why they were calling for this. I asked was something going on that I needed to know about. They advised me that he wasn't doing well. That he was losing weight and not eating and that they were seeing approaching signs of the end of life. Of course, this was devastating news.

When I heard this news, I began to cry, and I immediately began to feel and share my guilt. I was feeling guilty that I may not have gone to see him as much as I should have. I was feeling guilty that I may not have brought him home as much as I should have. The hardest part was realizing that I hadn't been to see him for over a month. Also, I was feeling guilty that the reason I hadn't been to see him for the last month was because I was hurt with him, all over again, about the way he treated us when we were children.

You see, one of his brothers had passed a month before. My youngest brother and I had gone to get him and took him to Huddle House, where he still loved to go, to tell him. Before he went to the nursing home, and when he was still able to drive and go, he went there every day to eat breakfast and dinner and he spent a large portion of his days there. He had made a lot of friends there, both workers and other members of the community. We hadn't been able to take him out for a while due to the cold, but it was a warm day, so we decided to tell him about his brother's passing while there. We told him and asked him if he thought he would be up to going. I explained that it was about a two-and-a-half-hour drive there and another two-and-a-half hours back, along with the time for the funeral. So, it would be a long day for him and us to take him. He said he didn't know if he would be able but that he would like to if he could. As we were leaving, we saw how much weaker he had become since the last time we had taken him out because he wasn't even able to lift his leg to get back in the vehicle. My brother and I had to pick him up to put him in the car. I realized at that time how difficult it would be to take him, but I was still going to leave it up to him. When we got back to the nursing home, I told him as we were leaving that I would check with him tomorrow and see if he thought he could go to the funeral. He had forgotten all about us telling him that his brother had passed, even though it had only been a little while since we had told him. I realized that he was unable to stand or lift his legs, and it was too much riding. Also, considering he would need to be changed and knowing he couldn't even stand, along with the fact that most of his day consisted of sleeping, which had become his favorite thing to do for the last few years.

It was a hard decision, but I felt it would be entirely too much
for him.

So, my two oldest brothers and I made the trip to the funeral. On the way home, we began sharing stories about our childhood, and I heard some stories I never knew that brought back a lot of the same hurt and pain that I relived in the first chapter of this book. The same hurt and pain, and now some new hurt and pain with stories I had never heard, that had caused me so much anguish that I quit writing for an entire year.

I was told about the day a hammer was thrown at one of my
brothers.

My brothers were working with my dad behind the house to build a fence. My brother made the comment that they wouldn't be working on the fence the next day because company was coming. It was going to be Easter Sunday, and some family was coming for Easter at our house, and we were all excited. Dad said to him, "I guess by God we will." My brother said, "Uh-uh, 'cause Jimmy and them are coming." Well, my brother's simple comment infuriated my dad so much that he hauled off and threw the hammer at him. My brother explained that he saw Dad raising his arm back to throw it at him, and he took off running. It hit him in the hip, and he still has pain from it to this day. He is in his early sixties, and the pain isn't just physical but also emotional, probably fifty years or so later. It was also both hurtful and emotional for me to hear about it for the first time, and it took me back to our childhood pain… as well.

My brother was referring to our double first cousins. One of Dad's brothers married one of Mom's sisters, and they had six kids also, all boys. Of all our cousins, we were closest to them, and we were all excited they were coming from Alabama to our house. This was the first time I knew anything about this, since I'm sure I was inside cleaning the house.

I was told about the day that same brother got beaten because he was too little to do what Dad was requiring him to do.

My brother explained that he was sitting on the couch and because he was little/young and he was sitting all the way back that his feet/shoes were in the couch. He said Dad told him to get his feet out of the couch. So, he scooted up to get his feet out of the couch, and Dad told him to sit back. So, he sat back, and of course, his feet/shoes went back into the couch because he was unable to do both. He couldn't sit back and keep his feet out of the couch, and he couldn't sit up to keep his feet out of the couch because Dad would tell him to sit back. Even though he was too young to keep his feet out of the couch when he sat back, he wasn't too young to remember the beating he got because of it.

I was told about the day that one of my younger brothers got beaten and thrown to the ground, and they thought he was dead.

My brothers told me of the day my dad was washing the car, and my brother, who was two years younger than me, was building a dam with rocks in the driveway to catch some water from the car being washed. My dad told him to stop, but he continued to build the dam with the rocks, just trying to catch some water. My brother who was telling me about this said that my younger brother was really young and was very little when this happened. He said that Dad got so mad that he went after him, and my younger brother saw him coming for him, and he took off running. He said my dad caught him, picked him up, beat the crap out of him, and then threw him on the ground. My oldest brother said he had to make my dad stop beating him. He said he just knew he was dead. My brother that this happened to is close to sixty, but tears filled his eyes, as well as mine, when we recently discussed this, and he relived the memory; these are still very painful memories for him, and it was a very painful story for me to hear.

We also talked and remembered the incident I shared earlier about the lighter being thrown at my sister and many more painful memories about our childhood.

So, the trip to my uncle's funeral was painful in more ways than one. Although we were feeling the sorrow of the loss of our uncle, we were also remembering a lot of hurt, pain, and sorrow of our youth.

Therefore, the guilt I was feeling on February 23 when I got the call from the nursing home was because I had been hurt with my dad for the last month for this pain that we were all still living with as a result of things that were done when we were children, and I hadn't been to see him as I should/would have.

Although I can't totally speak for my brothers, there was something that took place, of the questions for a reason, the hurt, the pain, and the suffering, when I realized that my dad was about to lose his life.

I know for me, the hurt I felt went out the window, and it became about my dad and the hurt and pain he was going through at this stage of life. Instead of harboring the hurt, it was replaced with love and forgiveness. It was the love and forgiveness that the Lord teaches by example for us to give one another. It was probably five days, almost to the minute, from the time I received the call from the nursing home to the time my dad passed, but what happened in those five days, and the days after until his funeral, I believe, is what the Lord wanted me to share with you about the difficulties that we can overcome if we will open up our hearts and **trust in Him to heal us of all of life's pains, sorrows, hurts, wrong decisions, and yes… sins!**

Wednesday, February 24

I left work and went to the nursing home and found my dad in the bed with the covers over his head, which was unusual. He was very weak and groggy and had deteriorated since I had seen him last, and it was hard to understand him most of the time. I was testing him to see how his mind was and asked him to tell his nurse who I was. He said my official name, which surprised me, instead of my nickname, which I thought he might do, or just say that I was his daughter. I thought, *Well, his mind is okay right now if he can do that.* My brother-in-law and his wife came, and he knew his name also but couldn't recall my sister-in-law's name but knew her face. I called my family to let them know what the nursing home had told me and that, according to what I saw, he may not even make it to his eighty-sixth birthday on Friday, February 26.

Thursday, February 25

I went to see him the next morning before going to work. He was still groggy, confused, and incomprehensible and didn't seem to know who I was when I asked him. But before I left, I told him that I would be back when I got off work. He did ask me what time that would be, and I told him around six o'clock. Surprisingly, he remembered me telling him I would be back at six because he asked if it was six o'clock already when I came in. I told him it was six o'clock and I was back like I told him I would be. I did, however, see a tremendous change in him from what I had seen on Wednesday as well as that morning. He was alert and talking better, although sometimes it was still hard to understand him. My two older brothers and a lot of other family members came that night. I was astonished and couldn't believe how he was compared to how he had been. He was cutting up, asking people to marry him and give him hugs, and was a completely different person. I began to think and was apologetic because I thought that I had given the family the wrong impression of how he was. We all had a wonderful visit with him that night, and before we left, we all shared a wonderful prayer with him. He was definitely experiencing the power surge you hear about, and we were fortunate enough to witness it.

Friday, February 26

Happy Birthday!

I decided to take the day off to spend his eighty-sixth birthday with him since I knew it would probably be his last. One of my brothers, who had spent the night with me because he lives one hour and a half away, and I went to see him the next morning, and we sang happy birthday to him. After we sang happy birthday to him, he also sang it to himself. I asked if he was hungry, and he said he was. I asked him if he wanted some eggs, and he said he wanted some bacon too. That was good to hear since they said he hadn't been eating anything, not even peanut butter and jelly sandwiches, which had become his favorite thing to eat for the last few years. Someone asked if he wanted to go smoke too, which was also one of his favorite things to do, but he had also stopped doing that, and he said, "H*** yeah." So, I went to get him the food he wanted, but unfortunately, they didn't have bacon… only sausage. His CNA, who was calling him Pawpaw, got him up and out of bed to eat, and they had a discussion about their pending marriage along with his pending marriage with every other woman who worked there who had jokingly agreed they would marry him. He was spry and cutting up, which was also good to see on his birthday. He made an inappropriate gesture to the CNA, who was making sure he was able to eat and chew his food without choking. He sang happy birthday to himself again, and he ate a few bites of eggs, picked up his toast by himself and ate a bite, and then ate a bite of sausage. He then said, "I'm ready to get back in that bed." The CNA asked if he was going to smoke, and he told her, "No, I'm ready to get back in that bed and die." The CNA said, "You ain't gonna do that… who told you that?" He said, "God." I was somewhat shocked at his calmness but also pleased because he seemed to be ready and embracing what was happening to him and apparently being prepared for it by the Lord. So, he was put back in the bed, as he had asked.

My two oldest brothers, who went to the funeral with me, said that he had told them on Thursday, when they were alone with him before all his other visitors got there that day, that he was ready to die.

He had several visitors on his birthday, and he was alert and cutting up and even took a hat from one of his granddaughter's husbands because it had red on it, which has always been his favorite color, and most of his attire consisted of red, including his socks.

That afternoon my brother and I just had finished the hospice paperwork, and the hospice nurse was on one side of him checking him, and I was standing on the other side. He looked directly at me and directly into my eyes and said, "Will you go with me?"

I wasn't sure what he was asking me to do, so I jokingly said, "Yes, not sure where we are going, but I will go."

He very sternly looked at me again and directly into my eyes again and asked me again, "Will you go with me?" So, with his sternness and him adamantly asking me for the second time, I believed in my heart the depth of what he was asking was if I would be with him when he passed. The hospice nurse asked him where he was going, and he abruptly and plainly said, "Gainesville."

I told him I would go with him, and I began to explain to the nurse he had been a trucker who had traveled all over. As I was explaining this to her, my heart and mind were thinking, *I believe he is asking me to be with him*, but if he had asked me to go to heaven, I might have hesitated… because I'm not ready to go. But with him asking me to go to Gainesville, I simply thought, *What better place in Georgia to refer to as heaven?* There are so many "-villes," but look at all the gains he will be receiving…

I felt his reference to Gainesville = Heaven!

As I was standing there in a room full of people, my mind was processing what had just happened and the beauty of it. I got brought back to reality by the hospice nurse telling me she wanted to speak to me in private. We went into the hall, and she shared that he needed to be on oxygen to help with the pneumonia and the COPD and explained some more about their plan of care.

Saturday, February 27

I got sick after leaving on Friday and lost my voice, so I didn't make it back until around lunch the next day. It was my goal to get some food in him. I was able to feed him an entire PB&J sandwich, two glasses of water, one cup of coffee, and some cake. I couldn't stand the thought of him not eating anything. Although I had to coach him into eating, swallowing, and drinking, he ate an entire sandwich except for one bite, which was more than he had in days. Since I was sick, I left and went back home with plans to go back and feed him dinner. I arrived at 5:30 p.m. and could see that he had declined since lunch and was only able to get half a sandwich in him, and he was choking and coughing so much that I finally had to give up.

Sunday, February 28

Two of his brothers came from Alabama to see him, and he knew their names and faces, just confused one for the other. My two oldest brothers, and one's wife, were there most of the day. He wasn't able to eat again due to choking and coughing, although I tried. I was only able to get him to eat another half a sandwich, but it was much harder than even the day before.

His brothers left around 3 p.m., and his nurse came in to check on him. She asked me if I was okay with her giving him some morphine. She explained she was only going to give him enough to make him comfortable. I explained that I was okay with whatever would be better and easier on him. I told her I could tell he was struggling, and he was having a hard time getting choked and coughing. She also explained that she was calling hospice to come and check on him. The hospice nurse sat down by me after checking him and said, "I'm sure you have some questions for me." I didn't really know what to ask but assumed she saw something she felt I needed to know, so I said, "I know that no one can tell when he may pass but in your professional opinion do you see a timeframe?" She explained that she did see that it was near and although she, of course, couldn't be sure, she would say twenty-four to seventy-two hours, but more like twenty-four. She explained that if there was anyone that wanted to see him before he would go, we needed to go ahead and notify them.

Monday, February 29

It was hard to leave him that night, but I knew I had to get some rest since I was sick and knew what was about to happen. My brother and I came to my house that night. I woke up a little before 3 a.m. and lay there for a while and couldn't go back to sleep for thinking about him. I called, and they said he was the same. I lay there until about 3:15 a.m. and decided to just get up and go because I wasn't doing any good just lying there. I didn't want to wake my brother, who was sleeping in my den just outside my bedroom, so I just got up and put on my boots and quietly tried to sneak out my bedroom door. When I came out, I saw that he wasn't in the bed. I went outside, thinking he would be on the porch smoking, and his vehicle was gone. I thought to myself, *Oh well, I guess I will meet him there.* I got there, and he came in right behind me because he had gone and gotten coffee. So, he and I sat there in the dimness of his room and watched him breathe and quietly talked. We both went out a few times for one thing or another… coffee, use the restroom, or smoke breaks for him. I was also keeping a check on his feet and legs and told my brother when they were getting cold. I remember being told, when Mom was passing, that cold feet and legs is a sign that it is happening and that the hearing is the last thing to go.

So, a few minutes after nine, my brother got up to go out for a smoke break. A few minutes after he left, I noticed that my dad seemed to be barely breathing and that the pulse was slowly diminishing in his neck, which we had been watching all night. I immediately went to the side of his bed and placed two fingers on his neck for his pulse and watched his breathing and knew that he was passing. I began to panic a little, knowing that it was happening and I was alone with him. I took my cell phone out to call my brother and was fumbling, trying to call him with one hand. I pushed the nurse call button, and the nurse came in, and I told him he was passing. He checked him and said he believed I was right, and before I knew what was happening, he said, "I'm going to call hospice," and he disappeared from sight. I thought to myself, *Now I'm alone again.* I tried calling my brother again, and his phone began ringing… in the room; he had left it.

So, reality sat in, and I realized that it was him and me; I realized that I was the only one with him, and it was up to me to take control of the situation or crumble under the pressure…

> *I calmly laid my hand on my father's hand and told him,*
> *"Dad, it's Trish. I'm here with you… like you asked me to be…*
> *and whenever you are ready… just go on and be with Jesus*
> *and Meemaw. I love you."*

As soon as I finished those words, I saw his tongue come up like he was trying to say something back to me, but then he let out his last breath. I felt he was trying to tell me that he loved me back… with his last breath.

> *It was so beautiful and peaceful. It was as beautiful and*
> *natural as childbirth.*

I was both honored and humbled to be there with him and to walk with him to the gates of Heaven… or Gainesville. Just as honored and humbled as I was to be with my mom.

I was also just as honored and humbled to speak at his funeral, or preach, as he had asked me to do a few days shy of six years earlier when I spoke at the passing of my sister.

The night before speaking, I sat down and prayed about what I would say. Below is the poem that transpired that I read and shared with everyone that day.

Pawpaw

Pawpaw was a man, who was born in 1930,
He was also a man that wasn't very wordy,
But we kids learned early on that when he spoke… we better
listen,
Or on our behinds… we would not be sittin'!

He married his wife Christine, who passed away in 1992,
But together, they had six kids, and I'm sure, at times, it may
have seemed like a zoo,
Four kids by age twenty-six for him… and twenty-three for
her,
I bet those years were mostly a blur,
Two more to come to add to the bunch,
I can't begin to even imagine… just trying to feed us lunch!

This may explain some things that went on in our youth,
'Cause one thing's for sure, we always ate good, and that's the
truth,
We always had gardens, and I mean gardens galore,
One up the road, one down the road, and even one across the
road next door,
We would work all day, hoeing row after row, but no matter
what we did, it seemed there was always one more!

He was also a man, who was a truck driver… both day and
night,
That's how he made his living and saw lots of sights,
He traveled this country from one end to the next,
Now… I wonder how often we heard from him… since back
then, there wasn't text!

And as far back as I'm sure we can all remember,
He disappeared every chance he got from October through
  December,
He would put on his camo and head for the woods,
There wasn't a question whether he could or if he should,
Didn't matter how long he sat or if he had any luck,
It was the thrill of the hunt and the wait for the buck!

He also sang a lot while he sat on his front porch swing,
And I'll never forget the most beautiful song, to me, I heard
  him sing,
He broke out in song as he sat there in the wind,
And he sang out loud, "Jesus, You Are My Only Friend."

So, one day I picked him up, for a visit, to bring him home,
And he broke out again with that song as we sat there alone,
So, I took that time to ask what he had on his mind,
About Jesus and his salvation and if he knew he would be in
  that line!

And because of that special time that we shared with each
  other that day,
I can stand here before you all and honestly say,
He went to heaven a mere five days ago!
And though we may love and miss him and his humor so,
I am so thankful that now we all know!
That Pawpaw is with Jesus and our other loved ones we
  knew,
And one day we will see them all again… when we go too!
And as Pawpaw would say… see ya sat'day!

Written on March 4, 2016, at 12:02 a.m.
In Loving Memory of Pawpaw

Before I read the poem above, I shared how easy it is to be saved by sharing the Romans Road.

> *Salvation that comes from trusting Christ—which is the message we preach—is already within easy reach.*
> — Romans 10:8, TLB

> *In fact, it says, "The message is very close at hand; it is on your lips and in your heart." And that message is the very message about faith that we preach: If you openly declare that Jesus is Lord and believe in your heart that God raised him from the dead, you will be saved. For it is by believing in your heart that you are made right with God, and it is by openly declaring your faith that you are saved.*
> — Romans 10:8–10 (NLT)

I shared earlier what reason number one was for this book. Therefore, the second reason for this book is **your salvation**!

It is as easy as the Romans Road shared above.

All the faith you need can be compared to the size of a mustard seed.

> *The Kingdom of Heaven is like a mustard seed planted in a field. It is the smallest of all seeds, but it becomes the largest of garden plants and grows into a tree where birds can come and find shelter in its branches.*
> — Matthew 13:31–32, NLT

By simply not choosing, you are making a terrible choice!

"No Jesus" — "No Peace"
"Know Jesus" — "Know Peace"

Therefore, since we have been justified through faith, we have peace with God through our Lord Jesus Christ.
— Romans 5:1, NIV

For many years I have said, "When I grow up, I want to work for the Lord." You have just read my first official written attempt at being grown up!

Again, I want to share the same quote from the prologue!

Perhaps this is the moment for which you were created.
— Esther 4:14

I believe this is the moment for which I was created.
Amen!

— In Christ,

Trish

CONNECT WITH TRISH

I have let some people read this book, prior to publication, that I consider some of my closest friends and confidants or that I have met throughout life, whether more recently, or are longtime friends from the distant past, or complete strangers that I have simply met by chance. As a result of my sharing my book with some of them, it has opened many doors for people to feel comfortable sharing their uncomfortable stories with me.

Therefore, I would like to send an open invitation to anyone who needs or wants to share their story as well. Everyone has a story, but not everyone feels comfortable sharing it with the world but would love to have someone to either just listen, share with, seek prayer, or simply let it go by releasing it.

Through my journey, I found it was very liberating, therapeutic, and extremely freeing to let all those past heartaches go!

My prayer has always been that by me sharing my uncomfortable stories, I may be helping someone, a few, or many have the courage they need by lending them a helping hand, an ear, and letting them know they are not alone or possibly leading them to Christ!

Please feel free to write me at:

Patricia Bagwell
1595 Pecan Grove Road
Washington, GA 30673

Photo compliments of Jordan and Morgan Perryman
of Beauty and Beard Photography, Augusta, Georgia

CPSIA information can be obtained
at www.ICGtesting.com
Printed in the USA
BVHW051151260623
666382BV00009B/189